crochet costume party

crochet costume party

Create simple and fun children's costumes for fairytale characters, animals, a superhero, and more

emma friedlander-collins

CICO BOOKS

LONDON NEW YORK

In memory of Claire Richardson

This edition published in 2024 by CICO Books
an imprint of Ryland Peters & Small Ltd
341 E 116th St, New York, NY 10029

www.rylandpeters.com

10 9 8 7 6 5 4 3 2 1

First published in 2015 as *Crochet Dress-Up*.

Text © Emma Friedlander-Collins 2024
Design, illustration, and photography
© CICO Books 2024

A CIP catalog record for this book is available
from the Library of Congress.

ISBN: 978 1 80065 330 6

Printed in China

Editor: Rachel Atkinson
Designer: Alison Fenton
Photographer: Terry Benson
Stylist: Robert Merrett
Illustrator: Stephen Dew

In-house editor: Jenny Dye
Art director: Sally Powell
Creative director: Leslie Harrington
Head of production: Patricia Harrington
Publishing manager: Carmel Edmonds

MIX
Paper from
responsible sources
FSC
www.fsc.org   FSC® C106563

contents

Introduction 6
Before you begin 8

the costumes 10

pete the pirate 12

Beard 14
Eye patch 15
Tricorn hat 16
Skull & crossbones motif 18
Parrot 20

little mermaid 22

Hair 24
Tail 26
Little crab 28

superhero 30

Mask 32
Cuffs 34
Chest plate 36

snow queen 38

Snowflake crown 40
Snowflake collar 42
Icicle cuffs 44

robin hood 46

Peaked hat 48
Arrow quiver 50
Wrist guards 52

forest fairy 54

Flower garland 56
Corsage 58
Fairy wings 59

cowboy carl (or carla) 62

Hat 64
Holster 66
Sheriff's badge 68

red riding hood 70

Hooded cape 72
Basket 74
Apple 76

pussy cat 78

Hat with cat ears 80
White-tipped tail 81

magic unicorn 82

Horn headdress 84
Swishy tail 85

vigo the viking 86

Helmet 88
Thor's hammer 90
Viking cuffs 91

rapunzel 92

Braided hair 94
Shrug 96

wicked witch 98

Black hat 100
Cobweb collar 102
Spider 104

wily wizard 106

Starry hat 108
Beard 110

gray rabbit 112

Hat with rabbit ears 114
White tail 115

Techniques 116
Crochet stitch conversion
   chart 126
Suppliers 126
Index 127
Acknowledgments 128

introduction

Once upon a time there was a craftaholic who loved all textiles, and spent all her free time wandering around haberdashers and yarn stores, mooning over the beautiful things. Now, when she was young she'd been taught how to knit, and she was just horrible at it. No matter how hard she tried or how much she practiced, she just couldn't help dropping stitches, adding stitches, and getting terribly muddled when it came to reading patterns, so she gave it up as a lost cause, but carried on mooning over yarn all the while.

One day, shortly after her first "little beast" was born, she was struck by the fact that she had never considered crochet. One hook, one ball of yarn, and some online tutorials later, an addiction was born. Desperate to make some super-cute and über-cool things for her little one to dress up in, she searched and searched but couldn't find anything to make, so she started designing her own pieces and writing her own patterns. With some gentle encouragement from her beloved, a little Etsy shop was set up under the name of "Steel & Stitch" and the patterns started selling worldwide.

This book is a collection of my original dressing-up pieces, all made for my sons—now big beast and little beast—their friends, and my nephews (and me, sometimes). The originals have all been worn many times, but because of the wonder of crochet they hold their shape, are soft enough for even the littlest ones, can be washed (VERY important if your beasts are anything like mine), and can mostly be made in a couple of hours.

before you begin

Here are a few things you need to know, and equipment you will need, before you start to crochet.

abbreviations

ch(s)	Chain(s)
ch-sp	Chain space
cm	Centimeter
dc	Double crochet
dc2tog	Double crochet 2 stitches together to decrease 1 stitch
dtr	Double treble crochet
g	Gram
hdc	Half double crochet
in	Inches
m	Meter
mm	Millimeter
oz	Ounce
pm	Place marker
rep	Repeat
RS	Right side of work
sc	Single crochet
sc2tog	Single crochet 2 stitches together to decrease 1 stitch
ss	Slip stitch
st(s)	Stitch(es)
t-ch	Turning chain
tr	Treble crochet
WS	Wrong side of work
yds	Yards

equipment

Craft wire: Used to give a few elements their shape, and to hold their structure.

Hooks: The following hooks are used in the projects.

US	UK
G/6	4mm
7	4.5mm
H/8	5mm
I/9	5.5mm
J/10	6mm
K/10½	7mm
L/11	8mm

Please note there is no direct US hook size conversion from 7mm, but we have suggested the nearest lower size (US K/10½). However you should adjust your hook size as necessary to achieve an even gauge.

Stitch markers: You will need a removable stitch marker for when you are working in spirals, to keep track of where each "round" of the spiral starts and ends. The pattern will tell you where to place the marker (pm) and it should be moved up as you complete each round. They come in all shapes and sizes, just ensure it is removable!

Tape measure: Always handy for making sure your finished outfit will fit the recipient.

Tapestry needle: A blunt ended needle with a large eye for sewing up and weaving in ends.

Yarn: There are two main thicknesses of yarn used in the projects, Light Worsted (DK) weight and Bulky (Chunky) weight. Please use the following yardage information as a guide when selecting your yarn:
Light Worsted (DK) weight: 328yds (300m) per 3½oz (100g)
Bulky (Chunky) weight: 153yds (140m) per 3½oz (100g)

You will also find additional specialty yarns featuring in a few of the projects, including the Mermaid and Unicorn. Details for these are given with each project.

The phrase "small quantity" is used for projects or features that tend to use less than 1oz (25g) of yarn. In some case you will only need a very small amount of a particular color.

pattern notes

Each costume has the yarn, hooks, and notions listed for each individual item, making it easy to mix and match different pieces from the various outfits. If you are making the full costume, please ensure you check how much yarn and what equipment you will need to complete it before you start.

skill level

Each project includes a star rating as a skill level guide and you will find the project includes the techniques listed below:

★ Projects for first-time crocheters, using basic stitches, with minimal shaping.

★★ Projects using basic stitches, repetitive stitch patterns, simple color changes, and simple shaping and finishing.

★★★ Projects using a variety of techniques, such as basic lace patterns or color patterns, mid-level shaping, and finishing.

the costumes

In the following pages you'll find full instructions for crocheting and making up the different elements of the costumes, plus helpful tips and suggestions for what else to wear to complete the look.

pete the pirate

BEARD • EYE PATCH • TRICORN HAT • SKULL & CROSSBONES MOTIF • PARROT

A short drive from where we live is a coastal town that has an annual "Pirate Day" to see if they can break the world record for the number of people dressed as a pirate. I'd only just learned to crochet when we decided to head over in all our pirate finery to be part of the event.

I looked around everywhere for a little crocheted skull and crossbones to sew onto my youngest son's outfit, but couldn't find quite the right one. The skull and crossbones is the first appliqué pattern I ever made and has since been used numerous times, for everything from babygrows to bunting. The next year a hat, beard, and eye patch followed, and then after some pleading from my eldest son, the parrot popped up to finish it off. This costume hasn't just been used for "Pirate Day"—we regularly dig it out for wearing to school on fancy dress days, or just at home when we're playing pirates on our bed-ship.

complete the look

You can get really carried away with this one and go for a full pirate-style white shirt, waistcoat, breeches, and striped socks, or keep it simple with a striped t-shirt, and a rolled-up pair of pants. The beard pattern could be used as part of a Viking outfit, or how about a bearded lady circus costume!

beard

A pirate needs a beard—just imagine trying to shave with a cut-throat razor on the high seas!

you will need

Yarn

Light Worsted (DK) weight:
1oz (25g) of Brown (or your color of choice)

Hooks & Notions

US 8/H (5mm) crochet hook
Tapestry needle

Gauge

Gauge is not critical but the fabric should be firm yet flexible.

Size

One size: To fit 4–7 years
6¹⁄₂in (16.5cm) wide x 4in (10cm) long (including mustache)

Abbreviations

See page 8.

pattern notes

You can easily adapt the beard to fit smaller or larger children by making the loops over the ears shorter or longer.

for the mustache

Leaving a long tail, make 30ch.
Row 1: Ss in second ch from hook, 1sc in next ch, 1hdc in next 2 ch, 1dc in next 2 ch, 1tr in next 2 ch, 1dtr in next 2 ch, 1tr in next ch, 1dc in next ch, 1hdc in next ch, 1sc in next ch, ss in next ch, 1sc in next ch, 1hdc in next ch, 1dc in next ch, 1tr in next ch, 1dtr in next 2 ch, 1hdc in next 2 ch, 1dc in next 2 ch, 1hdc in next 2 ch, 1sc in next ch, ss in last ch.
Fasten off, leaving a long tail.

for the beard

Leaving a long tail, make 23ch.
Row 1: 1dc in fourth ch from hook, 1dc in each st to end, turn. (21 sts)
Row 2: 3ch (counts as 1dc now and throughout), 1dc in next 9 sts, 3dc in next st, 1dc in next 10 sts, turn. (23 sts)
Row 3: 3ch, 1dc in next 19 sts, 1sc in next 3 sts, turn.
Row 4: Sc2tog, 1dc in next 19 sts, sc2tog. (21 sts)
Row 5: 1ch (does not count as a st), dc2tog, 1dc in next 17 sts, dc2tog, 1sc in next st, 1ch, turn. (19 sts)
Row 6: 1ch (does not count as a st), *dc2tog, 1dc in next st; rep from * a further five times, ss in last st to finish. (13 sts)
Fasten off, leaving a long tail.

finishing

Using the long tails from the beard, sew the corners of the beard to the mustache and tie the long tails on the mustache to make loops to hook over your pirates' ears.

eye patch

Every self-respecting pirate wears his scars—and his eye patch—with pride.

you will need

Yarn
Light Worsted (DK) weight:
Small quantity of Black

Hooks & Notions
US G/6 (4mm) crochet hook
Tapestry needle

Gauge
Gauge is not critical but adjust the hook size to produce a firm fabric.

Size
One size:
Patch: 2¼ x 1¼in (5.5 x 3cm)
Ties: Adjust to fit

Abbreviations
See page 8.

for the patch

Row 1: Make a magic ring and ss to secure. Work 1ch, 5sc into ring. Keeping the sts as a semicircle, pull the starting tail tight, turn. (5 sts)
Row 2: 3ch, 1dc in base of ch, 2dc in each st to end, turn. (10 sts)
Row 3: 3ch, 1dc in base of ch, 1dc in next st, *2dc in next st, 1dc in next st; rep from * a further 3 times. (15 sts)
Row 4 (ties): Make 90ch (or length required).
Fasten off.
Rejoin yarn at opposite end of the patch, make 90ch (or to match the first tie).
Fasten off.

finishing

Weave in ends (see page 124). Use the chain ties to secure the patch around your little pirate's head.

tricorn hat

This traditional hat tops off the outfit. Add the skull and crossbones motif (page 19) to scare your enemies!

Add the skull and crossbones motif (page 19)

pattern notes

To make a smaller hat, omit Round 7.

To make a bigger hat, work an additional row after Round 7, working an extra 1dc every sixth stitch to give you 48 sts at the end.

you will need

Yarn

Bulky (Chunky) weight:
2¾oz (75g) of Black

Fingering (4ply) weight:
Small amount of Gold metallic for edging

Note: If you can't find a metallic yarn, substitute it with an alternative Fingering (4ply) weight yarn in a contrast color.

Hooks & Notions

US L/11 (8mm) crochet hook
Tapestry needle

Gauge

Gauge is not critical but adjust the hook size to produce a firm fabric.

Size

One size: To fit 4–7 years
22in (56cm) circumference

Abbreviations

See page 8.

for the hat

Round 1: Make a magic ring and ss to secure. Work 6sc into ring, ss in first sc to join. (6 sts)

Round 2: 3ch, 1dc in base of ch, 2dc in each st to end, ss in third ch of t-ch to join. (12 sts)

Round 3: 3ch, 1dc in base of ch, 1dc in next st, *2dc in next st, 1dc in next st; rep from * a further four times, ss in third ch of t-ch to join. (18 sts)

Round 4: 3ch, 1dc in base of ch, 1dc in next 2 sts, *2dc in next st, 1dc in next 2 sts; rep from * a further four times, ss in third ch of t-ch to join. (24 sts)

Round 5: 3ch, 1dc in base of ch, 1dc in next 3 sts, *2dc in next st, 1dc in next 3 sts; rep from * a further four times, ss in third ch of t-ch to join. (30 sts)

Round 6: 3ch, 1dc in base of ch, 1dc in next 4 sts, *2dc in next st, 1dc in next 4 sts; rep from * a further four times, ss in third ch of t-ch to join. (36 sts)

Round 7: 3ch, 1ch in base of ch, 1dc in next 5 sts, *2dc in next st, 1dc in next 5 sts; rep from * a further four times, ss in third ch of t-ch to join. (42 sts)

Rounds 8–12: 3ch, 1dc in each st to end, ss in third ch of t-ch to join.

Do not fasten off and continue for the Brim as follows:

Round 13: 3ch, 1dc in base of ch, 1dc in next 4 sts, *2dc in next st, 1dc in next 4 sts; rep from * a further six times, 2dc in next st, 1dc in last st, ss in third ch of t-ch to join. (51 sts)

Round 14: 3ch, 1dc in base of ch, 1dc in next 4 sts, *2dc in next st, 1dc in next 4 sts; rep from * a further eight times, 2dc in last st, ss in third ch of t-ch to join. (62 sts)

Round 15: 3ch, *2dc in next st, 1dc in next 4 sts; rep from * a further eleven times, 2sc in last st, ss in third ch of t-ch to join. (75 sts)

Round 16: 3ch, *2dc in next st, 1dc in next 4 sts; rep from * a further thirteen times, 2sc in next st, 1sc in next 3 sts, ss in third ch of t-ch to join. (90 sts)

Round 17: 3ch, 1dc in each st to end, ss in third ch of t-ch to join.

Make three, short flat sections in your circle for the "corners" as follows:

Round 18: 3ch, 1dc in each of next 21 sts, 1sc in next st, ss in next 5 sts, 1sc in next st; *1dc in each of next 22 sts, 1sc in next st, ss in next 5 sts, 1sc in next st; rep from * once more, 1sc in last st. Fasten off.

Weave in all loose ends (see page 124).

finishing

Join gold metallic thread at any edge stitch, work 1ch, 1sc in each st around, ss in first sc to join. Fasten off. Shape the hat as follows:

Find the center of each flattened section (the middle slip stitch of the five slip stitches worked in Round 18). Fold them together, lifting the brim up around the body of the hat to form the three corners of your Tricorn Hat. Take a short length of yarn and using the tapestry needle, put a few stitches through each corner to keep each side together. Using a little more yarn, sew a few more stitches through the lifted brim to the body of the hat to keep it up and ensure it keeps its shape.

skull & crossbones motif

This skull and crossbones can be made in a larger size (see Pattern Notes, below) to adorn a flag, or to pin on a jacket.

you will need

Yarn
Light Worsted (DK) weight:
Small quantity of White

Hooks & Notions
US G/6 (4mm) crochet hook
Tapestry needle

Gauge
Gauge is not critical but adjust the hook size to produce a firm fabric.

Size
One size:
Skull: 1½ x 2in (4 x 5cm)
Crossbones: 1½ x 1in (4 x 2.5cm)

Abbreviations
See page 8.

for the skull

Row 1: 8ch, 1dc in fourth ch from hook, 1dc in next 4 sts, turn. (5 sts)
Row 2: 3ch, 1dc in each st to end.
These are the teeth.
Continue as follows to form the eye sockets:
Row 3: 8ch, miss 1 st, 1sc in next st, 8ch, ss in last st, turn.
Continue as follows to complete the skull:
Row 4: 3ch, [2dc, 2tr, 3dtr] around 8ch-sp, 1dtr in sc, [3dtr, 2tr, 3dc] in next 8ch-sp.
Fasten off.

for the crossbones (make 2)

Make 13ch, ss in fourth ch from hook, 3ch, ss in same ch as before, ss down the chain, 3ch, ss in end of original chain, 3ch, ss in same ch as before. Fasten off.

finishing

Join bones together in the middle, then sew them on with a couple of stitches at the bottom corners of the skull.
Sew in place on the tricorn hat or wherever you like!

pattern notes
Make this motif in smaller or larger sizes by simply changing the thickness of the yarn and using a hook size suited to it. It is perfect for using up oddments of yarn from your stash.

parrot

Polly Parrot knows where the "pieces of eight" are buried—but will she tell you?

you will need

Yarn

Light Worsted (DK) weight:
1oz (25g) of (**A**) Red
Small quantities of (**B**) White and (**C**) Yellow

Hooks & Notions

US I/9 (5.5mm) crochet hook

Small amount of toy stuffing

Two ¼in (0.5cm) black beads plus needle and thread to match

Removable stitch marker

Tapestry needle

Gauge

Gauge is not critical but adjust the hook size to produce a firm fabric.

Size

One size:
5½in (14cm) tall (excluding feet)

Abbreviations

See page 8.

for the head

Round 1: Using A, make a magic ring and ss to secure. Work 5sc into ring, ss in first sc to join. (5 sts)
Round 2: 1ch, 2sc in each st, ss in first sc to join. (10 sts)
Round 3: 1ch, *2sc in next st, 1sc in next st; rep from * a further four times. (15 sts)
Round 4: 1ch, *2sc in next st, 1sc in next 2 sts; rep from * a further four times. (20 sts)
Rounds 5–9: 1ch, 1sc in each st to end.
Round 10: *Sc2tog, 1sc in next 2 sts; rep from * a further four times, ss in first sc to join. (15 sts)
Round 11: *Sc2tog, 1sc in next st; rep from * a further four times, ss in first sc to join. (10 sts)
Stuff the head and continue as follows:
Round 12: [Sc2tog] five times. (5 sts)
Round 13: [Sc2tog] twice, 1sc, ss in first sc to join.
Fasten off, leaving a long tail for sewing the head to the body.

for the eyes (make 2)

Using B, make a magic ring and ss to secure. Work 6sc into ring, ss in first sc to join. Fasten off.
Use the tails to sew the eyes to either side of the head.

for the beak

Using C, make 4ch.
Row 1: 1sc in second ch from hook, 1sc in next 2 ch, turn. (3 sts)
Row 2: 1ch, 1sc in next 2 sts, turn. (2 sts)
Row 3: 1ch, 1sc in next st.
Fasten off, leaving a long tail. Use the tail to sew the beak to the head.
Weave in loose ends (see page 124).

for the body

Round 1: Using A, make 12ch, ss in first ch to join taking care not to twist the sts.

Rounds 2–3: 1ch, 1sc in each ch, ss in first sc to join. (12 sts)

Round 4: 1ch, *1sc in next 3 sts, 2sc in next st; rep from * twice more, ss in first sc to join. (15 sts)

Round 5: 1ch, 1sc in each st around, ss in first sc to join.

Round 6: 1ch, *1sc in next 4 sts, 2sc in next st; rep from * twice more, ss in first sc to join. (18 sts)

Round 7: 1ch, 1sc in each st around, ss in first sc to join.

Round 8: 1ch, *1sc in next 5 sts, 2sc in next st; rep from * twice more, ss in first sc to join. (21 sts)

Round 9: 1ch, 1sc in each st around, ss in first sc to join.

Round 10: 1ch, *1sc in next 6 sts, 2sc in next st; rep from * twice more, ss in first sc to join. (24 sts)

Round 11: 1ch, *1sc in next 7 sts, 2sc in next st; rep from * twice more, ss in first sc to join. (27 sts)

Round 12: 1ch, *1sc in next 3 sts, sc2tog; rep from * a further four times, 1sc in last 2 sts, ss in first sc to join. (22 sts)

Round 13: 1ch, *1sc in next 2 sts, sc2tog; rep from * a further four times, 1sc in last 2 sts, ss in first sc to join. (17 sts)

Round 14: 1ch, *1sc in next st, sc2tog; rep from * a further four times, 1sc in last 2 sts, ss in first sc to join. (12 sts)

Stuff the body and continue as follows:

Round 15: [Sc2tog] six times, ss in first sc to join. (6 sts)

Round 16: [Sc2tog] three times, ss in first sc to join. Fasten off.

Securely sew the head onto the open end of the body.

for the tail

Using A, make 8ch.

Row 1: 1sc in second ch from hook, 1sc in each st to end, turn. (7 sts)

Row 2: 1ch, 1sc in each st across, turn.

Rows 3–5: 3ch, 1dc in each st across, turn.

Row 6: *4ch, 1dtr in next st, 4ch, ss in next st; rep from * twice more. Fasten off. This creates the three feathers.

Row 7: Join C in fourth ch of t-ch on Row 6. Work 3ch, 1dtr in next st, 3ch, ss in top of last st in current feather. Fasten off. Repeat for remaining feathers.

for the wings (make 2)

Using A, make 9ch.

Row 1: 1sc in second ch from hook, 1sc in next 6 ch, 3sc in last ch. (10 sts)

Row 2: Working up the other side of foundation ch, 1sc in next 7 sts, 2sc in end ch, ss in first sc of Row 1 to join. (19 sts)

Work in rounds as follows:

Round 1: 1ch, 1sc in next 9 sts, [1sc, 1dc, 1sc] in next st, 1sc in the next 9 sts, ss in first sc to join. (21 sts)

Round 2: 1ch, 2sc in next st, 1sc in next 9 sts, [1sc, 1dc, 1sc] in next st, 1sc in next 10 sts, ss in first sc to join. (22 sts)

Fasten off.

finishing

Sew the tail and wings onto the body and weave in all ends (see page 124).

Pop the beads in the middle of the eye circles securing with the needle and thread, then with a whistle and a "pretty Polly" your parrot is all finished!

little mermaid

HAIR • TAIL • LITTLE CRAB

This was a costume inspired by a little girl who LOVES dressing up and was desperate to be a mermaid. She had played with some of the other dress-up crochet and her mom approached me the next day and said: "You know, Ava would be thrilled if you could make a mermaid costume." Well, I only usually have boys to make things for, so I grabbed the chance to make something girly. The tail pays homage to granny chic and the classic granny square, which is the first thing I ever learned to crochet. The mermaid hair is still one of my favorite makes ever— in fact I made it just big enough for me to wear.

hair

These long locks in seaweed colors will make your mermaid look as if she has just stepped out of the sea.

pattern notes

For a smaller size, omit Rounds 3, 5, and the two sets of 5 ss.

you will need

Yarn

Bulky (Chunky) weight:
100g (3½oz) each of (**A**) Teal, (**B**) Mint, and (**C**) Turquoise
Metallic Fingering (4ply) weight:
1oz (25g) of (**D**) Dark green

Note: If you can't find a metallic yarn, substitute it with an alternative Fingering (4ply) weight yarn in a suitable color.

Hooks & Notions

US L/11 (8mm) crochet hook
Tapestry needle

Gauge

Gauge is not critical but the fabric should be firm yet flexible.

Size

One size: To fit 4–7 years
20in (51cm) circumference

Abbreviations

See page 8.

for the hair

Round 1: Using A, B, C, and D held together as one strand, make a magic ring and secure with ss. Work 6sc into ring, ss in first sc to join. (6 sts)

Round 2: 3ch (counts as 1dc now and throughout), 1dc in base of ch, 2dc in each st around, ss in third ch of t-ch to join. (12 sts)

Round 3: 3ch, 1dc in base of ch, 1dc in next st, *2dc in next st, 1dc in next st; rep from * a further four times, ss in third ch of t-ch to join. (18 sts)

Round 4: 3ch, 1dc in base of ch, 1dc in next 2 sts, *2dc in next st, 1dc in next 2 sts; rep from * a further four times, ss in third ch of t-ch to join. (24 sts)

Round 5: 3ch, 1dc in base of ch, 1dc in next 3 sts, *2dc in next st, 1dc in next 3 sts; rep from * a further four times, ss in third ch of t-ch to join. (30 sts)

Rounds 6–7: 1ch, 1sc in each st around, ss in first sc to join.
Do not fasten off and continue as follows to create the hair:

Steps 1–9: *Make 51ch, 1sc in second ch from hook, 1sc in each ch, 1sc in next st of hat brim to secure; rep from * a further nine times.

Step 10: Ss in next 5 sts along the edge of the hat.

Steps 11–19: *Make 41ch, 1sc in second ch from hook, 1sc in each ch, 1sc in next st of hat brim to secure; rep from * a further nine times.

Step 20: Ss in next 5 sts along the edge of the hat.
Fasten off.

finishing

Create a center parting along the top of the hair as follows:
Take the 10 longer strands and part them in the middle.
Bring the fifth one on each side around to the back, ensuring that the four remaining strands of the bundle are held underneath them, and secure together at the side and back of the hat with a few stitches.

tail

Pick as many colors from the ocean as you like to make the mermaid's tail—it's perfect for using up oddments from your stash.

you will need

Yarn

Bulky (Chunky) weight:
100g (3½oz) each of (**A**) Teal, (**B**) Mint, and (**C**) Turquoise

Hooks & Notions

US K/10½ (7mm) crochet hook

Co-ordinating ribbon—¾in (2cm) wide x 80in (203cm) long

Tapestry needle

Gauge

Gauge is not critical but the fabric should be firm yet flexible.

Size

One size: To fit ages 4–7
20in (51cm) circumference

Abbreviations

See page 8.

for the tail

Row 1: Using C, make 53ch, 1dc in fourth ch from hook, 1dc in each st to end, turn. (51 sts)

Rows 2–6: 3ch (counts as 1dc now and throughout), 1dc in each st across, turn.

Fasten off C.

Row 7: Join B, 3ch, 2dc in same st, *1ch, miss 2 sts, 3dc in next st; rep from * a further 16 times, 3ch, ss in third ch of t-ch in Row 6. Fasten off B. (17 granny sts)

Row 8: Join A in top of last dc of previous row, turn. 3ch, *3dc in ch-sp, 1ch; rep from * a further fifteen times, 3ch, ss in third ch of t-ch in row below. Fasten off A. (16 granny sts)

Row 9: Join C in top of last dc of previous row, turn. 3ch, *3dc in ch-sp, 1ch; rep from * a further fourteen times, 3ch, ss in third ch of t-ch in row below. Fasten off C. (15 granny sts)

Row 10: Join B in top of last dc of previous row, turn. 3ch, *3dc in ch-sp, 1ch; rep from * a further thirteen times, 3ch, ss in third ch of t-ch in row below. Fasten off B. (14 granny sts)

Row 11: Join A in top of last dc of previous row, turn. 3ch, *3dc in ch-sp, 1ch; rep from * a further twelve times, 3ch, ss in third ch of t-ch in row below. (13 granny sts)

Row 12: Join C in top of last dc of previous row, turn. 3ch, *3dc in ch-sp, 1ch; rep from * a further eleven times, 3ch, ss in third ch of t-ch in row below. (12 granny sts)

Row 13: Join B in top of last dc of previous row, turn. 3ch, *3dc in ch-sp, 1ch; rep from * a further ten times, 3ch, ss in third ch of t-ch in row below. (11 granny sts)

Row 14: Join A in top of last dc of previous row, turn. 3ch, *3dc in ch-sp, 1ch; rep from * a further nine times, 3ch, ss in third ch of t-ch in row below. (10 granny sts)

Row 15: Join C in top of last dc of previous row, turn. 3ch, *3dc in ch-sp, 1ch; rep from * a further eight times, 3ch, ss in third ch of t-ch in row below. (9 granny sts)

Row 16: Join B in top of last dc of previous row, turn. 3ch, *3dc in ch-sp, 1ch; rep from *a further seven times, 3ch, ss in third ch of t-ch in row below. (8 granny sts)

Row 17: Join A in top of last dc of previous row, turn. 3ch, *3dc in ch-sp, 1ch; rep from * a further six times, 3ch, ss in third ch of t-ch in row below. (7 granny sts)

Row 18: Join C in top of last dc of previous row, turn. 3ch, *3dc in ch-sp, 1ch; rep from * a further five times, 3ch, ss in third ch of t-ch in row below. (6 granny sts)

Row 19: Join B in top of last dc of previous row, turn. 3ch, *3dc in ch-sp, 1ch; rep from * a further four times, 3ch, ss in third ch of t-ch in row below. (5 granny sts)

Row 20: Join A in top of last dc of previous row, turn. 3ch, *3dc in ch-sp, 1ch; rep from * a further three times, 3ch, ss in third ch of t-ch in row below. (4 granny sts)

Row 21: Join C in top of last dc of previous row, turn. 3ch, *3dc in ch-sp, 1ch; rep from * twice more, 3ch, ss in third ch of t-ch in row below. (3 granny sts)

Row 22: Join B in top of last dc of previous row, turn. 3ch, *3dc in ch-sp, 1ch; rep from * once more, 3ch, ss in third ch of t-ch in row below. (2 granny sts)

Row 23: Join A in top of last dc of previous row, 3ch, 3dc in ch-sp, 3ch, ss in corner st of previous row to finish.

fins (make 2)

Round 1: Using C, make 16ch, 1sc in second ch from hook, *1sc in next ch, 1hdc in next 2 ch, 1dc in next 2 ch, 1tr in next ch, 1dtr in next ch, 1tr in next ch, 1dc in next 2 ch, 1hdc in next 2 ch, 1sc in next ch, 1sc in last ch; working down opposite side of the chain, 1sc in first ch; rep from * once more.

Round 2: Working around the previous row, 2sc in first st, *1sc in next 7 sts, 2sc in next st; rep from * twice more, 1sc in next 6 sts. Fasten off.
Work the edging as follows:

Round 3: Join B, work *2ch, ss in next st; rep from * to end.
Fasten off.

finishing

Attach the fins either side of the final granny stitch of the mermaid tail.
Weave in all ends and block gently according to the ball band (see page 124).
Take the ribbon and weave it in and out of the top row of double crochet stitches of the tail, leaving a good even length at each side. Thread each length across the edges (as though lacing your shoes) and attach to your little mermaid.

little crab

This cute little crab completes the mermaid's outfit—
you can pin it to the tail, or leave it loose to be carried.

you will need

Yarn

Light Worsted (DK) weight:
Small quantity of Red

Hooks & Notions

US G/6 (4mm) crochet hook
Small amount of toy stuffing
Two black beads
Black embroidery floss
Needle and black sewing thread
Tapestry needle

Gauge

Gauge is not critical but adjust the
hook size to produce a firm fabric.

Size

One size: 1in (2.5cm) across
(excluding claws)

Abbreviations

See page 8.

for the body

Round 1: Make a magic ring and secure with ss. Work 4sc into ring, ss in first sc to join. (4 sts)
Round 2: 1ch, 2sc in each st around, ss in first sc to join. (8 sts)
Round 3: 1ch, *2sc in next st, 1sc in next st; rep from * a further three times, ss in first sc to join. (12 sts)
Round 4: 1ch, 1sc in each st around, ss in first sc to join.
Round 5: [Sc2tog] six times, ss in first sc to join. (6 sts)
Stuff the body.
Round 6: [Sc2tog] three times, ss in first sc to join. (3 sts)
Fasten off and use the tail to close the small opening.

for the legs (make 6)

Make 6ch.
Fasten off, leaving a long tail.

for the claws (make 2)

Make 8ch, 1sc in fifth ch from hook, 1ch, ss to finish.
Fasten off, leaving a long tail.

finishing

Using the long tails, sew the legs and claws onto the body.
Weave the ends in through the legs and into the body (see page 124), pulling them tightly to give them their shape.
Securely sew the beads on for eyes (see page 125) and add a few stitches for the mouth.

pattern notes

The legs and claws are made separately then sewn into the body of the crab later, so when you fasten off, leave long tails for stitching with.

superhero

MASK • CUFFS • CHEST PLATE

Having two boys of my own, and four nephews, all between the ages of two and eight years, there's a lot of superhero play that goes on. The hero mask was one of the first real costume pieces that I ever made, and very quickly there were requests from all the little boys in my life. This really is the single most worn costume in our house, partly because my youngest wore it every day for a whole summer, but also because the mask doubles up as a winter hat. The good thing is, because it's made of yarn they can fall asleep wearing it in the back of the car, and it isn't uncomfortable.

complete the look

Pajamas are perfect for this, or use a t-shirt and sweat pants. Underpants over the top are optional!

mask

This mask does double duty as a hat—useful when my youngest refuses to wear one, which is most days!

you will need

Yarn

Bulky (Chunky) weight:
2oz (50g) of (**A**) Electric blue

Light Worsted (DK) weight:
Small quantity of (**B**) White

Hooks & Notions

US G/6 (4mm) crochet hook
US I/9 (5.5mm) crochet hook
Tapestry needle

Gauge

Gauge is not critical but adjust the hook size to produce a firm fabric.

Size

One size: To fit 4–7 years
18½in (47cm) circumference

Abbreviations

See page 8.

for the mask

Round 1: Using A and 5.5mm (US I/9) hook, make a magic ring and secure with ss. 3ch (counts as 1dc now and throughout), work 11dc into ring, ss in third ch of t-ch to join. (12 sts)

Round 2: 3ch, 1dc in base of ch, 2dc in each st around, ss in third ch of t-ch to join. (24 sts)

Round 3: 3ch, 1dc in base of ch, 1dc in next st, *2dc in next st, 1dc in next st; rep from * to end, ss in third ch of t-ch to join. (36 sts)

Round 4: 3ch, 1dc in base of ch, 1dc in next 2 sts, *2dc in next st, 1dc in next 2 sts; rep from * to end, ss in third ch of t-ch to join. (48 sts)

Rounds 5–12: 3ch, 1dc in each st around, ss in third ch of t-ch to join.

Round 13: 3ch, 1dc in next 10 sts, 1ddc in next st, 1dtr in next st, 10ch, miss 6 sts, 1dtr in next 2 sts, 10ch, miss 6 sts, 1dtr in next st, 1tr in next st, 1dc in each st to end.
(36 sts and two 10ch-sp eyeholes)

pattern notes

Adjust the size to fit 2–3 years by omitting Round 4.

To make the hat a little bit stretchier, use a US K/10½ (7mm) crochet hook and omit Round 4.

Round 14: 3ch, 1dc in each st to eyeholes, 8dc around the whole chain (rather than through the sts), 1dc in each st between the eyes, 8dc around second eyehole chain, 1dc in each of next 5 sts, dc2tog, 1dc in next 5 sts, dc2tog, 1dc in next 5 sts, dc2tog, ss in third ch of t-ch to join.
Fasten off.

for the star motif
Using B and US G/6 (4mm) hook, make 3ch, ss in first ch to make a ring.

Round 1: 1ch, 10sc into the ring. (10 sts)
Round 2: *5ch, ss in second ch from hook, 1sc in next ch, 1hdc in next ch, 1dc in last ch, miss 1 st, ss in next st; rep from * a further 4 times.
Fasten off, leaving a long tail.

finishing
Use the long tail of the star motif to stitch it to the mask at the center front between the eyeholes. Weave in all loose ends (see page 124).

cuffs

When you're wrestling with evil, you need to protect yourself. These superhero cuffs will do the job.

you will need

Yarn

Bulky (Chunky) weight:
1½oz (38g) of (**A**) Electric Blue
Light Worsted (DK) weight:
Small quantity of (**B**) White

Hooks & Notions

US I/9 (5.5mm) crochet hook
Tapestry needle

Gauge

Gauge is not critical but adjust the hook size to produce a firm fabric.

Size

One size: To fit 4–7 years—
see pattern notes
Length: 5¼in (13.5cm)
Circumference: 6in (15cm)

Abbreviations

See page 8.

for the cuffs (make 2)

Using yarn A, make 18ch.
Row 1: 1dc in fourth ch from hook, 1dc in each ch to end, turn. (16 sts)
Rows 2–12: 3ch (counts as 1dc now and throughout), working into the back loop only 1dc in each st to end, turn. Fasten off, leaving a long tail.

for the fins (make 6)

Using A, make 5ch, ss in second ch from hook, 1sc in next st, 1hdc in next st, 3dc in next st.
Fasten off, leaving a long tail.

for the star motif (make 2)

Follow the instructions for the Star Motif on page 33.

finishing

Using the long tails, attach three fins in a line down the center of each cuff, then sew the star motif in place. Sew the long edges together. Weave in all loose ends (see page 124).

pattern notes

Create superhero forearm shields by making a longer starting chain.

Make these for younger or older children by working fewer or more repeats of the double crochet row.

chest plate

Every hero needs to have his own symbol on his chest, to be instantly recognized by enemies and grateful humans alike.

you will need

Yarn
Bulky (Chunky) weight:
75g (2¾oz) of (**A**) Electric Blue
Light Worsted (DK) weight:
Small quantity of (**B**) White

Hooks & Notions
US G/6 (4mm) crochet hook
US I/9 (5.5mm) crochet hook
Tapestry needle

Gauge
Gauge is not critical but adjust the hook size to produce a firm fabric.

Size
One size: To fit 4–7 years—
see pattern notes on page 35
Chest: 26in (66cm) circumference

Abbreviations
See page 8.

for the chest plate

Using A and US I/9 (5.5mm) hook, make 81ch.
Row 1: 1sc in second ch from hook, 1sc in each st to end, turn. (80 sts)
Rows 2–11: 1ch, 1sc in each st across, turn.
Fasten off, leaving a long tail.

for the straps (make 2)

Using A and US I/9 (5.5mm) hook, make 7ch.
Row 1: 1sc in second ch from hook, 1sc in each st to the end, turn. (6 sts)
Row 2: 1ch, 1sc in each st across, turn.
Fasten off, leaving a long tail.

for the star motif (make 1)

Follow the instructions for the Star Motif on page 33.

finishing

Sew the short sides of the plate together. Lie the chest plate flat, with the center seam facing you. Attach each strap to the chest plate approximately 8 sts from the center seam. Miss 14 sts and attach the other end of the strap to chest plate. Stitch the star motif to the center front of the chest plate. Weave in all loose ends (see page 124).

snow queen

SNOWFLAKE CROWN • SNOWFLAKE COLLAR • ICICLE CUFFS

We were snowed in a couple of winters ago and my boys and I started looking for winter stories to read. *The Snow Queen* by Hans Christian Andersen was one of my favorites as a child, so I dug out my old book of fairy tales and we read it together. My eldest asked if we could "play" Snow Queen and this outfit is what popped into my head.

This is the first time I ever thought to crochet using two yarns together, as I knew I needed the sturdiness of a regular yarn but really wanted something sparkly too. As I couldn't find a suitable single yarn, I bought two—one sparkly and one regular, then crocheted holding them together as one strand. The result had just the right level of "cold and icy" that I'd been looking for.

complete the look

This pattern caught the eye of our neighbors' daughter who trotted over in a very pretty, white lace bridesmaid's dress, put all these on, and went off to play in the park. You may not have a spare bridesmaid's dress lying around, but a simple white or pale blue cotton dress makes a perfect Snow Queen gown.

snowflake crown

A crown made from snowflakes is perfect for the queen of winter.

you will need

Yarn

Light Worsted (DK) weight:
Small quantity of White

Metallic Fingering (4ply) weight:
Small quantity of White or Silver

Note: If you can't find a metallic yarn, substitute it with an alternative Fingering (4ply) weight yarn in a suitable color.

Hooks & Notions

US 7 (4.5mm) crochet hook

Tapestry needle

Gauge

Gauge is not critical but adjust the hook size to produce a firm fabric.

Size

One size: To fit 4–7 years

18in (46cm) circumference

Abbreviations

See page 8.

for the snowflake motif (make 3)

Make 5ch, ss in first ch to join in a ring.

Round 1: 3ch, working into center of ring make 1dc, *3ch, 2dc; rep from * a further three times, ss in third ch of t-ch to join.

Round 2: 1ch, 1sc in third ch of t-ch, *[1sc, 5ch, 1sc] in 3ch-sp, miss 1 dc, 1sc in next st; rep from * a further four times, ss in first sc to join.

Round 3: *3ch, [ss, 5ch, ss, 3ch, sl st] in 5ch-sp, ss in next st, ss in center sc**, ss in 5ch-sp; rep from * a further four times, ending last repeat at **.

Fasten off, leaving a long tail.

for the band

Leaving a long tail, make 37ch. Work 1dc in fourth ch from hook, 1dc in each ch to the end. Fasten off, leaving a long tail.

finishing

Lay the snowflakes side-by-side with two points at the bottom and one at the top—like a star—and sew the two bottom points touching one another together using the long tails. Sew each end of the band to each end of the row of snowflakes. Weave in all loose ends and block gently according to the ball band (see page 124).

pattern notes

All elements for the Snow Queen outfit are worked holding the two yarns (white and metallic) together throughout. If preferred, you can find a suitable sparkly yarn and use that instead.

snowflake collar

This snowflake collar is so pretty you could wear it over any old sweater, and it would make it look magical.

you will need

Yarn

Light Worsted (DK) weight:
Small quantity of White

Metallic Fingering (4ply) weight:
Small quantity of White or Silver

Note: If you can't find a metallic yarn, substitute it with an alternative Fingering (4ply) weight yarn in a suitable color.

Hooks & Notions

US 7 (4.5mm) crochet hook

36in (90cm) white ribbon

Tapestry needle

Gauge

Gauge is not critical but adjust the hook size to produce a firm fabric.

Size

One size: 12½in (32cm) long (excluding ribbon)

Abbreviations

See page 8.

for the snowflake motif (make 5)

Using the pattern for the Snowflake Motif on page 40, make five snowflakes.

finishing

Join the motifs together in a row as instructed for the Crown on page 40.
Block gently according to the ball band (see page 124).
Loop the ribbon through either end of the row of snowflakes and tie with a bow on your Snow Queen.

pattern notes

All elements for the Snow Queen outfit are worked holding the two yarns (white and metallic) together throughout. If preferred, you can find a suitable sparkly yarn and use that instead.

icicle cuffs

These pretty wristbands are tied together with ribbon that is woven through the crochet pieces, like laces.

you will need

Yarn

Light Worsted (DK) weight:
Small quantity of White

Metallic Fingering (4ply) weight:
Small quantity of White or Silver

Note: If you can't find a metallic yarn, substitute it with an alternative Fingering (4ply) weight yarn in a suitable color.

Hooks & Notions

US 7 (4.5mm) crochet hook

36in (90cm) white ribbon

Tapestry needle

Gauge

Gauge is not critical but adjust the hook size to produce a firm fabric.

Size

One size: 4¾in (12cm) wide, 5in (12.5cm) deep (excluding finger loop and ribbon)

Abbreviations

See page 8.

for the cuffs (make 2)

Make 28ch.
Row 1: 1dc in eighth ch from hook, *4ch, miss 3 ch, 1dc in next ch; rep from * to end, turn.
Row 2: 5ch, 1dc in first ch-sp, *4ch, 1dc in next ch-sp; rep from * to end, turn.
Repeat Row 2 twice more.
Fasten off.

for the snowflake motif (make 2)

Using the pattern for the Snowflake Motif on page 40, make two snowflakes, leaving a long tail as you fasten off.

finishing

Sew a snowflake to the middle of the long edge of the mesh band—attach with the two points opposite the finger loop.
Weave in all loose ends.
Block gently according to ball band (see page 124).
Cut the ribbon in half and use a length for each cuff. Lace the ribbon through the mesh at either short end of the cuff in criss-crosses (just like shoe laces). Tie them in a bow on your Snow Queen's wrists.

pattern notes

All elements for the Snow Queen outfit are worked holding the two yarns (white and metallic) together throughout. If preferred, you can find a suitable sparkly yarn and use that instead.

robin hood

PEAKED HAT • ARROW QUIVER • WRIST GUARDS

This is a costume I actually forced on the beasts! I loved the Disney movie version of *Robin Hood* when I was little—Robin was a charming fox and Little John a big ol' daddy bear, and even though I tried to get them to love it too, they still prefer more modern movies. Armed with a shiny new crochet hook and chunky green yarn, I thought I could possibly convert them with a quick costume, and once we put some arrows in the quiver, tied the wrist guards on, and popped a feather in the hat, they were away.

complete the look

An oversized green t-shirt and a brown belt are all you need to finish this off, but don't forget your bow and arrows!

peaked hat

Robin's hat, in leafy green, provides great camouflage among the trees of Sherwood Forest—or your backyard.

you will need

Yarn

Bulky (Chunky) weight:
3½oz (100g) of Forest Green

Hooks & Notions

US J/10 (6mm) crochet hook
Removable stitch marker
Tapestry needle

Gauge

Gauge is not critical but adjust the
hook size to produce a firm fabric.

Size

One size: To fit 4–7 years

20in (51cm) circumference (before
brim); 24in (56cm) after brim;
9in (23cm) tall (with brim folded)

Abbreviations

See page 8.

for the hat

Round 1: Make a magic ring and secure with ss. 3ch (counts
as 1dc now and throughout), work 5dc into ring, ss in third
ch of t-ch to join. (6 sts)
Round 2: 2ch, 1dc in base of ch, 2dc in each st around,
ss in third ch of t-ch to join. (12 sts)
Round 3: 3ch, 1dc in base of ch, 1dc, *2dc in next st,
1dc; rep from * to end, ss in third ch of t-ch to join. (18 sts)

Round 4: 3ch, 1dc in base of ch, 2dc,
*2dc in next st, 2dc; rep from * to end,
ss in third ch of t-ch to join. (24 sts)

Round 5: 3ch, 1dc in base of ch, 3dc,
*2dc in next st, 3dc; rep from * to end,
ss in third ch of t-ch to join. (30 sts)

Round 6: 3ch, 1dc in base of ch, 4dc,
*2dc in next st, 4dc; rep from * to end,
ss in third ch of t-ch to join. (36 sts)

Round 7: 3ch, 1dc in base of ch, 5dc,
*2dc in next st, 5dc; rep from * to end,
ss in third ch of t-ch to join. (42 sts)

Round 8: 3ch, 1dc in base of ch, 6dc,
*2dc in next st, 6dc; rep from * to end,
ss in third ch of t-ch to join. (48 sts)

Rounds 9–13: 3ch, 1dc in each st to end,
ss in third ch of t-ch to join.

Round 14: 3ch, 1dc in base of ch, 3dc,
*2dc in next st, 3dc; rep from * to end,
ss in third ch of t-ch to join. (60 sts)

Round 15: 3ch, 1dc in base of ch, 4dc,
*2dc in next st, 4dc; rep from * to end,
ss in third ch of t-ch to join. (72 sts)

Round 16: 3ch, 1dc in base of ch, 5dc,
*2dc in next st, 5dc; rep from * around,
ss in third ch of t-ch to join. (84 sts)
Do not break yarn and continue as follows
in rows to create the Peak:

for the peak

Row 1: 3ch, 11dc, turn. (12 sts)
Row 2: 1ch, miss 1 st, 1sc in next st, 8dc,
1sc in next st, miss 1 st, ss in next st. (10 sts)
Fasten off.

finishing

Weave in all ends (see page 124). Using the
tapestry needle threaded with a length of
yarn, turn up the brim either side of the
peak and secure it in the body of the hat
with a few stitches.

arrow quiver

Robin and his band of outlaws need their arrows ready to hand for when the Sheriff of Nottingham approaches.

you will need

Yarn

Bulky (Chunky) weight:
1¾oz (50g) of (**A**) Brown
Small quantity of (**B**) White

Hooks & Notions

US K/10½ (7mm) crochet hook
Removable stitch marker
Tapestry needle

Gauge

Gauge is not critical but adjust the hook size to produce a firm fabric.

Size

One size:
Quiver: 9½in (24cm) tall x
4in (10cm) diameter
Strap: 16½in (42cm)
circumference—adjust to fit

Abbreviations

See page 8.

for the quiver

Round 1: Using A, make a magic ring and secure with ss. Work 1ch, 6sc into ring, ss in first sc to join. (6 sts)
Round 2: 3ch (counts as 1dc now and throughout), 2dc in each st around to marker, ss in third ch of t-ch to join. (12 sts)
Round 3: 3ch, *2dc in next st, 1dc in next st; rep from * around, ss in third ch of t-ch to join. (18 sts)
Round 4: 3ch, *2dc in next st, 1dc in next 2 sts; rep from * around, ss in third ch of t-ch to join. (24 sts)
Round 5: 1ch, working in the back loop only work 1sc in each st around, ss in first sc to join.
Work in spirals (no turning chains required), keeping track of each round with the stitch marker and continue as follows:
Rounds 6–31: 1sc in each st around.
Fasten off A.
Round 32: Join B, 1sc in each st around, fasten off B.
Round 33: Rejoin A, 1sc in each st around, ss in first sc to join. Fasten off.

strap

Using A, make 110ch.
Rows 1–2: 1sc in second ch from hook, 1sc in each ch to end, fasten off A, turn.
Row 3: Join B, 1ch, 1sc in each st around, ss in first sc to join. Fasten off.

finishing

Using A and the tapestry needle, join the short ends of the strap together and attach to the body of the quiver.
Weave in all loose ends (see page 124).

wrist guards

These wrist guards are super-simple to make, but they really complete the look, and protect the archer's arms!

you will need

Yarn

Bulky (Chunky) weight:
Small quantities of (**A**) Forest Green, and (**B**) Dark Brown

Hooks & Notions

US J/10 (6mm) crochet hook
Tapestry needle

Gauge

Gauge is not critical but the fabric should be firm yet flexible.

Size

One size: To fit 4–7 years
6in (16.5cm) circumference;
4½in (12.5cm) tall

Abbreviations

See page 8.

for the wrist guards (make 2)

Using A, make 15ch.
Row 1: 1dc in third ch from hook, 1dc in each st to end, turn. (13 sts)
Rows 2–10: 3ch, 1dc in each st to end, turn.
Fasten off and weave in all ends.

finishing

Cut twelve 8in (20cm) lengths of B and make ties to attach to the wrist guards as follows:
Fold in half and use the crochet hook to pull the folded end through the fabric, then pass the cut ends through the loop to secure. Secure one at the top, middle, and bottom of either side of the wrist guards and tie the guards around the arms of your Merry Man or Maid Marian.

forest fairy

FLOWER GARLAND • CORSAGE • FAIRY WINGS

I will confess straight away that neither the flower garland nor the wings were made for anyone other than myself! Every year we go to a celebratory Spring festival where everyone wears flower garlands in their hair. I wanted something pretty, that wouldn't get damaged, and that I could use year after year—crochet seemed the perfect solution. It's so pretty and is comfortable to wear too. The wings followed on from the garland, and are just beautiful! One of the neighbors' daughters came in and begged to wear them, and now they double up as a decoration for my craft room, and dress-up for her.

complete the look

A cotton summer dress is all you need to complete this outfit. If your fairy has a favorite dress, you can pick yarn for the flowers in colors to match.

flower garland

No need to pick flowers from the forest or garden for this costume, just wear this pretty little garland in your hair.

you will need

Yarn

Light Worsted (DK) weight: Small quantities of (**A**) Bright Green, (**B**) Dark Green, (**C**) Light Green), (**D**) Yellow, (**E**) Pink, (**F**) Peach, and (**G**) White

Hooks & Notions

US G/6 (4mm) crochet hook
Tapestry needle

Gauge

Gauge is not critical but adjust the hook size to produce a firm fabric.

Size

One size: To fit 4–7 years— see pattern notes
18in (45cm) circumference

Abbreviations

See page 8.

for the band

Using A and B held together and leaving
a long tail, make 70ch.
Work 1sc in second ch from hook,
1sc in each st to end.
Fasten off, leaving a long tail.

for the flowers

Make 10 in the following color
combinations—4 using D at the center and E for
the petals, 3 using D at the center and F for the
petals, 3 using G at the center and D for the petals.
Work as follows:

Round 1: Using center color, make 5ch, ss in first
ch to join.

Round 2: 1ch, 10sc around the ch. Fasten off
center color.

Rounds 3–7: Join petal color, *(1sc, 1dc, 1sc)
in next st, ss in next st; rep from * a further four
times. Five petals made.

for the leaves

Make 50 in the following colors—14 using A,
26 using B, 10 using C.
Work as follows:
Make 7ch, 1sc in second ch from hook, 1hdc in next
st, 1dc in next st, 1tr in next st, 5dc in next st, working
down the opposite side of the chain 1tr in next 2 sts,
1dc in next st, 1hdc in next st, 1sc in next st.
Fasten off, leaving a long tail for sewing together later.

finishing

Using at least two leaves in B to give the flowers
a dark background to stand out against, take five
leaves and lay them in a star shape so the tips/edges
are all touching and sew them together. Place a flower
at the center and sew it securely in place. Make
a total of ten flower and leaf clusters and attach them
to the band. Tie the ends of the band together, weave
in all loose ends (see page 124), and pop it on the
head of your fairy.

pattern notes

The garland can be made to fit
anyone, just ensure the starting chain
for the band is long enough to go
comfortably around their head.

I like to crochet yarns together for a more organic
look. All you need to do is hold your yarns together
and crochet using them as one strand.

Play with color and make the flowers and leaves
whatever colors you like! Tonal versions would
be pretty or go wild using odds and ends
from your stash for a Technicolor look.

corsage

This cluster of flowers matches the garland, and doubles as a pretty anklet.

you will need

Yarn

Light Worsted (DK) weight:
Small quantities of (**A**) Bright Green, (**D**) Yellow, (**E**) Pink, (**F**) Peach, and (**G**) White

Hooks & Notions

US G/6 (4mm) crochet hook
Tapestry needle

Gauge

Gauge is not critical but adjust the hook size to produce a firm fabric.

Size

One size: 5¼in (13cm) circumference

Abbreviations

See page 8.

for the band

Using A, make 25ch.
Row 1: 1sc in second ch from hook, 1sc in each ch to end, turn.
Rows 2–6: 1ch, 1sc in each st to end, turn.
Fasten off.

for the flowers and leaves

Using the pattern for the Garland on page 56, make 3 flowers and 1 leaf.

finishing

Sew the leaf to the base and then sew the flowers on top of it, sew together the short sides of the base, weave in ends (see page 124), and then pop this on your fairy's wrist.

pattern notes

The corsage is adjustable to fit fairies of all ages! Just ensure the starting chain for the band is long enough to comfortably go around their wrist.

fairy wings

Make these to be worn, or just to look pretty hanging up in a little girl's (or a grown up's) shabby-chic bedroom.

you will need

Yarn

Small quantities of various yarns including Bulky (Chunky), Worsted (Aran), DK (Light Worsted), novelty yarns, and metallic thread held with the main yarn as you work

Hooks & Notions

US G/6 (4mm) crochet hook

US I/9 (5.5mm) crochet hook

Two wire coat hangers

Wire cutters

Duct tape or similar strong tape

Tapestry needle

2½ yds (2m) white ribbon

Gauge

Gauge is not critical but adjust the hook size to produce a firm fabric.

Size

One size: To fit 4 years and upward

Each wing is 5½ x 15in (14 x 38cm)

Abbreviations

See page 8.

for the frame (make 2)

Using the wire cutters, clip the hook off the coat hanger at the shoulder curve. Using duct tape, overlap and bind the ends together to create the frame for the wings. It can be bent and stretched into whatever shape you like.

Using bulky yarn and the larger hook, work single crochet around the frame hooking around the wire to cover it. Fasten off and weave in the loose ends (see page 124).

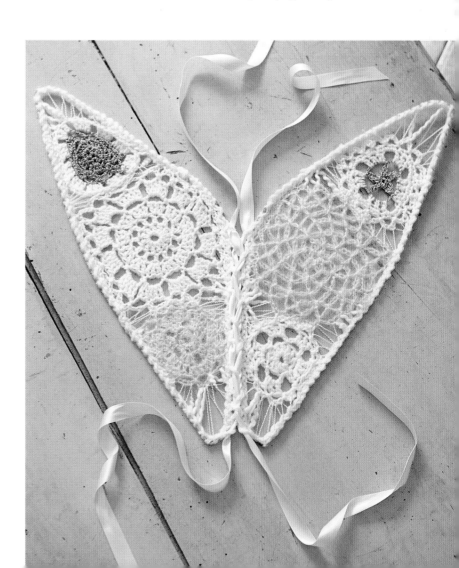

for the motifs

This is where you can get creative and play around creating various motifs to fill the inside of the wing frame. Mix different yarn weights, colors, textures, and motifs for a shabby-chic look, or keep everything uniform by duplicating the same motif—it's entirely up to you!

I used three motifs in each wing: Motifs 1–3 in Wing One and Motifs 2, 3, and 4 in Wing Two.

Motif 1

Make 6ch, ss in first ch to join.
Round 1: 3ch, 11dc in ring. (12 sts)
Round 2: *4ch (counts as 1dc and 1ch), [1dc, 1ch] in each st around, ss in third ch of t-ch to join.
Round 3: 3ch (counts as 1dc), 2dc in base of ch, 3dc in each st around, ss in third ch of t-ch to join.
Round 4: *5ch, miss 2 sts, ss in next st; rep from * a further 11 times.
Round 5: Ss in 5ch-sp, 3ch, 4dc in same ch-sp, 3ch, [5dc, 3ch] in each ch-sp around, ss in third ch of t-ch to join.
Round 6: *5ch, ss in third dc of 5dc in Round 5, 5ch, ss to 3ch-sp, rep from * around. Fasten off.

Motif 2

Make 5ch, ss in first ch to join.
Round 1: 1ch, 10sc in ring. (10 sts)
Round 2: *3ch, miss 1 st, ss in next st; rep from * a further four times.
Round 3: Ss into 3ch-sp, 3ch, 2dc in same ch-sp, 1ch, [3dc, 1ch] in each 3ch-sp around, ss in third ch of t-ch to join. (15 sts and 5 ch-sps)
Round 4: 3ch, and counting the ch-sps as sts, *1dc in next st, 2dc in next st; rep from * around. (30 sts)
Round 5: *5ch, miss 1 st, ss in next st; rep from * around.
Fasten off.

Motif 3

Make 5ch, ss in first ch to join.
Round 1: *5ch, ss in ring; rep from * a further three times, 3ch, 1dtr in ring.
Round 2: *3ch, ss in 5ch-sp; rep from * a further four times.

Round 3: *3ch, 2dc in same ch-sp, 2ch, *3dc in ch-sp, 2ch; rep from * around, ss in third ch of t-ch to join.
Round 5: *1ch, work 1sc in each st and 2sc in each ch-sp around, ss to first sc to join.
Round 7: *5ch, miss 1 st, ss in next stitch; rep from * around.
Fasten off.

Motif 4

Make 5ch, ss in first ch to join.
Round 1: *5ch, ss in ring; rep from * a further three times, 2ch, 1dtr in ring.
Round 2: *7ch, ss in third ch of 5ch-sp; rep from * a further three times, 3ch, 1dtr in third ch of 5ch-sp (at the base of 7ch).
Round 3: *5ch, ss in 4th ch of 7ch-sp; rep from * a further three times, 2ch, 1dtr in fourth ch of 5ch-sp (at the base of 7ch).
Rep Rounds 2 and 3 to make the motif as large as desired.

finishing

I made three motifs per wing, but you can do as many or as few as you like. For one wing lay motifs 1, 2, and 3 inside your wing frame—the largest in the center and the smaller two at either end.

Using the tapestry needle and a length of yarn, sew the edges touching the frame in place to the frame covering.
Repeat for the other wing using motifs 1, 2 and 4.
Using scraps of yarn, start at the frame edge, stitch in the gaps between the circles.

straps

To make loops for the ribbon straps, work as follows: For the right-hand wing only, join yarn at the top of the outside edge of the frame, *3ch, ss in next st; rep from * a further nine times. (10 loops made)
Rep for left-hand wing, lining the loops up to match the right-hand wing.
Take two lengths of ribbon and lace them between the wings into the loops as though you are lacing up shoes.

cowboy carl (or carla)

HAT • HOLSTER • SHERIFF'S BADGE

This is another one of those patterns that was in my head for ages and I was nervous about starting it, as I thought it might be really complicated. As it turned out, this was in fact all finished and done within a couple of hours and is one of the single most pleasing makes ever! The big beast loves wearing it, and the gun holster and badge were requests to make up a complete costume to play in. I'm extremely tempted to make a larger version of this hat for me to wear in the winter, and have already been asked by my sister if I can make one for her...and she is 34!

complete the look

A checked shirt, pair of jeans, and a belt are all you need to finish off this costume. If you happen to have a scrap of fabric lying around that would make a good neckerchief, then all the better.

hat

Yeehaw! I'm not quite sure if this is a Stetson or a Ten-Gallon, but every cowboy needs a hat.

pattern notes

The center of the hat is made in single crochet stitches to give a sturdy shape to the middle of the hat. The remainder is worked in double crochet stitches to keep the brim more flexible and easier to shape.

you will need

Yarn

Bulky (Chunky) weight:
3½oz (100g) of Tan

Hooks & Notions

US I/9 (5.5mm) crochet hook
Tapestry needle

Gauge

Gauge is not critical but adjust the hook size to produce a firm fabric.

Size

One size: To fit 4–7years
21in (53cm) circumference

Abbreviations

See page 8.

for the hat

Make 13ch.

Set-up: Work 2dc in fourth ch from hook, 1dc in next 8 sts, 5dc in end ch. Working up the other side of the foundation chain, 1dc in next 8 sts, 2dc in last st, ss in third ch of t-ch to join. (26 sts) Working in the round, continue as follows:

Round 1: 3ch (counts as 1dc now and throughout), 2dc in next 2 sts, 1dc in next 8 sts, 2dc in next 2 sts, 1dc, 2dc in next 2 sts, 1dc in next 9 sts, 2dc in next 2 sts, ss in third ch of t-ch to join. (34 sts)

Round 2: 1ch, 1sc in each st around, ss in first sc to join. (34 sts)

Round 3: 1ch, 1sc, 2sc in next st, 1sc in next 14 sts, 2sc in next st, 1sc in next st, 2sc in next st, 1sc in next 14 sts, 2sc in next st, ss in first sc to join. (38 sts)

Round 4: 1ch, 1sc, 2sc in next st, 1sc in next 16 sts, 2sc in next st, 1sc in next st, 2sc in next st, 1sc in next 16 sts, 2sc in next st, ss in first sc to join. (42 sts)

Round 5: 1ch, 1sc, 2sc in next st, 1sc in next 18 sts, 2sc in next st, 1sc in next st, 2sc in next st, 1sc in next 18 sts, 2sc in next st, ss in first sc to join. (46 sts)

Round 6: 3ch, 1dc in each st around, ss in third ch of t-ch to join.

Round 7: 3ch, 1dc in next 18 sts, 2dc in next st, 1dc in next 6 sts, 2dc in next st, 1dc in next 19 sts, ss in third ch of t-ch to join. (48 sts)

Round 8: 3ch, 1dc in next 18 sts, 2dc in next st, 1dc in next 8 sts, 2dc in next st, 1dc in last 19 sts, ss in third ch of t-ch to join. (50 sts)

Round 9: 3ch, 1dc in next 2 sts, 2dc in next st, 1dc in next 42 sts, 2dc in next st, 1dc in last 3 sts, ss in third ch of t-ch to join. (52 sts)

Round 10: 3ch, 2dc in next st, 1dc in next 23 sts, 2dc in next st, 1dc in next st, 2dc in next st, 1dc in next 24 sts, ss in third ch of t-ch to join. (55 sts)

Rounds 11–14: 3ch, 1dc in each st around.

Round 15: 3ch, *1dc in next 5 sts, 2dc in next st; rep from * to end, ss in third ch of t-ch to join. (64 sts)

Round 16: 3ch, *1dc in next 6 sts, 2dc in next st; rep from * to end, ss in third ch of t-ch to join. (73 sts)
Round 17: 3ch, *1dc in next 7 sts, 2dc in next st; rep from * to end, ss in third ch of t-ch to join. (82 sts)
Round 18: 3ch, *1dc in next 8 sts, 2dc in next st; rep from * to end, ss in third ch of t-ch to join. (91 sts)
Round 19: 3ch, *1dc in next 9 sts, 2dc in next st; rep from * to end, ss in third ch of t-ch to join. (100 sts)
Fasten off.

finishing

Weave in all loose ends (see page 124). Using A, secure the sides of the brim to the hat at either side. Shape the top of the hat by tucking the central single crochet area down into the middle a little bit and secure with a few stitches if required.

holster

This holster also makes a handy extra pocket.

you will need

Yarn
Bulky (Chunky) weight:
1¼oz (35g) of Tan

Hooks & Notions
US I/9 (5.5mm) crochet hook
Tapestry needle
Belt to wear your holster on

Gauge
Gauge is not critical but adjust the hook size to produce a firm fabric.

Size
One size: 4½in (11.5cm) wide x 8½in (21.5cm) tall

Abbreviations
See page 8.

for the holster

Make 19ch.

Row 1: 1sc in second ch from hook, 1sc in each ch to end, turn. (18 sts)

Rows 2–3: 1ch, 1sc in each st to end, turn.

Row 4: 1ch, 2sc in next st, 1sc in next 16 sts, 2sc in last st, turn. (20 sts)

Row 5: 1ch, 2sc in next st, 1sc in next 18 sts, 2sc in last st, turn. (22 sts)

Rows 6–11: 1ch, 1sc in each st to end, turn.

Row 12: 1ch, sc2tog, 1sc in next 18 sts, sc2tog, turn. (20 sts)

Row 13: 1ch, 1sc in each st to end, turn.

Row 14: 1ch, 2sc in the next st, 1sc in next 18 sts, 2sc in last st, turn. (22 sts)

Row 15: 1ch, 1sc in each st to end, turn.

Row 16: 1ch, 2sc in next st, 1sc in next 20 sts, 2sc in last st, turn. (24 sts)

Row 17: 1ch, 1sc in each st to end, turn.

Row 18: 1ch, 2sc in next st, 1sc in next 22 sts, 2sc in last st, turn. (26 sts)

Rows 19–22: 1ch, 1sc in each st to end, turn.

Row 23: 1ch, 2sc in next st, 1sc in next 24 sts, 2sc in last st, turn. (28 sts)

Row 24: 1ch, 2sc in next st, 1sc in next 26 sts, 2sc in the last st, turn. (30 sts)

Rows 25–26: 1ch, 1sc in each st to end, turn.

Row 27: 1ch, sc2tog, 1sc in next 18 sts, turn. Do not fasten off!

Work the belt loops as follows:

Rows 28–32: 1ch, 1sc in next 4 sts, turn.

Row 33: 1ch, 1sc in next 4 sts.
Fasten off. One belt loop created.

Rows 34–39: Rejoin yarn to Row 27, one st along from the previous loop, and repeat Rows 28–33.

Rows 40–45: Repeat Rows 34–39.
Fasten off.

finishing

Weave in all loose ends (see page 124). Fold fabric in half lengthwise and seam, creating a pocket for the Sheriff's gun.

sheriff's badge

If you want to keep the baddies out of Dodge, then you'll need a badge so everyone knows you're the sheriff.

you will need

Yarn

Bulky (Chunky) weight:
Small quantity of Light Gray

Hooks & Notions

US I/9 (5.5mm) crochet hook
Tapestry needle
Safety pin

Gauge

Gauge is not critical but adjust the hook size to produce a firm fabric.

Size

One size: 2½in (6.5cm) wide from point to point

Abbreviations

See page 8.

for the badge

Round 1: Leaving a long tail, make a magic ring and ss to secure. Work 6sc into ring, ss in first sc to join. (6 sts)

Round 2: 2sc in each st around. (12 sts)

Round 3: *4ch, ss in second ch from hook, 1sc in next st, 1hdc in next st, miss 1 st, ss in next st; rep from * a further five times. Fasten off.

finishing

Use the long tail from the magic ring to sew the safety pin to the back of the badge. Weave in all loose ends (see page 124).

pattern notes

To give the badge a metallic look, hold a strand of sparkly thread with the yarn as you work.

red riding hood

HOODED CAPE • BASKET • APPLE

Oddly, although a really simple and quick pattern, this is one of "those ones" that took ages to work out the best way to make it. I'd been asked by a friend if I could make a cape and this is the first thing that came to mind, but I spent months making and ripping back subtly different versions. I'd take it on the train, to the park, in the office on my lunch breaks, until finally I got it right. I think it's exceptionally cute and was well worth the work. The apple is one of the first amigurumi that I ever made and was a gift for a friend who had never seen woollen fruit before—she was extremely tickled to have it!

complete the look

Any pretty dress would look super cute with this little hood, whether in winter or summer.

hooded cape

Super sweet and equally cozy, this can double up as a winter warmer, as well as a costume.

you will need

Yarn

Bulky (Chunky) weight:
5¼oz (150g) of Red

Hooks & Notions

US K/10½ (7mm) crochet hook
Tapestry needle

Gauge

Gauge is not critical but adjust your hook to produce a flexible fabric.

Size

One size: To fit 4–7 years
Neck: 14in (35cm) circumference worn with 3in (7.5cm) positive ease
Length: 17¾in (45cm) from top of head to base of cape

Abbreviations

See page 8.

for the cape

Row 1 (RS): Make 42ch, 1dc in fourth ch from hook, *1dc in next 5 ch, 2dc in next ch, miss next ch; rep from * a further four times, 1dc in last 3 ch, turn. (40 sts)

Row 2: 3ch (counts as 1dc now and throughout), *1dc in next 5 sts, 2dc in next st; rep from * a further five times, 1dc in last 3 sts, turn. (46 sts)

Row 3: 3ch, *1dc in next 6 sts, 2dc in next st; rep from * a further five times, 1dc in last 3 sts, turn. (52 sts)

Row 4: 3ch, *1dc in next 7 sts, 2dc in next st; rep from * a further five times, 1dc in last 3 sts, turn. (58 sts)

Row 5: 3ch, *1dc in next 8 sts, 2dc in next st; rep from * a further five times, 1dc in last 3 sts, turn. (64 sts)

Row 6: 3ch, *1dc in next 9 sts, 2dc in next st; rep from * a further five times, 1dc in last 3 sts, turn. (70 sts)

Row 7: 3ch, *1dc in next 10 sts, 2dc in next st; rep from * a further five times, 1dc in last 3 sts, 2ch, turn. (76 sts)

pattern notes

The main cape section is made first and the hood worked afterwards. If you prefer, the hood can be made separately and sewn on.

To fasten the cape you can leave long tails when starting, or alternatively thread a ribbon through the stitches for a fancier fastening.

Row 8: 3ch, *1dc in next 11 sts, 2dc in next st; rep from * a further five times, 1dc in last 3 sts, turn. (82 sts)

Row 9: 3ch, *1dc in next 12 sts, 2dc in next st; rep from * a further five times, 1dc in last 3 sts, 2ch, turn. (88 sts)

Row 10: 3ch, *1dc in next 13 sts, 2dc in next st; rep from * a further five times, 1dc in last 3 sts, 2ch, ss in third ch of t-ch to finish. (94 sts)
Fasten off.

for the hood

With RS facing, rejoin yarn at the right-hand edge.
Work into the starting chain of cape as follows:

Row 1 (RS): 3ch, 1dc in each st across, turn. (40 sts)

Row 2: 3ch, *1dc in next 5 sts, 2dc in next st; rep from * a further five times, 1dc in last 3 sts, turn. (46 sts)

Rows 3–17: 3ch, 1dc in each st to end, turn.

Row 18: 3ch, 1dc in each st across.
Fasten off.

finishing

Seam the top edges of the hood together.
Weave in all loose ends and block gently according to the ball band (see page 124).
Use the remaining long tails to fasten around the neck. Alternatively, make chain lengths and sew to the cape or thread a ribbon through for a pretty finish.

skill level ★ ★

basket

This rustic-looking basket could be used by all sorts of fairytale characters, as well as Red Riding Hood.

you will need

Yarn
Bulky (Chunky) weight:
1oz (25g) of Dark Brown

Hooks & Notions
US I/9 (5.5mm) crochet hook
Removable stitch marker
Tapestry needle

Gauge
Gauge is not critical but adjust your hook to produce a firm fabric.

Size
One size:
12in (30.5cm) circumference
(at widest part);
9in (23cm) tall (including handle)

Abbreviations
See page 8.

for the basket

Round 1: Make a magic ring and secure with ss. Work 6sc into ring, ss in first sc to join, pm. (6 sts) Working in spirals, moving the marker up as you work, continue as follows:

Round 2: 2sc in each st to end. (12 sts)

Round 3: *2sc in next st, 1sc in next st; rep from * around. (18 sts)

Round 4: *2sc in next st, 1sc in next 2 sts; rep from * around. (24 sts)

Round 5: *2sc in next st, 1sc in next 3 sts; rep from * around. (30 sts)

Round 6: *2sc in next st, 1sc in next 4 sts; rep from * around. (36 sts)

Work in rounds as follows:

Round 7: 3ch, working in the back loop only 1dc in each st around, ss in third ch of t-ch to join. (36 sts)

Rounds 8–11: 3ch, 1dc in each st around, ss in third ch of t-ch to join. (36 sts)

Round 12: 1ch, 1sc in each st around.

Round 13: 1ch, working in the front loop only 1sc in each st around.

Do not fasten off and continue as follows to create the handle:
With hook still in ch from last round, make 31ch.
Miss 18 sts, ss into edge of basket to join handle to body of basket. 1ch, work sc back along the chain handle, ss back into body of the basket to finish.
Fasten off.

finishing

Weave in all loose ends (see page 124).

(see page 124)

pattern notes

The basket is worked on a small hook to give it strength and to hold the shape.

Use the stitch marker to indicate start of rounds when working in spirals, moving the stitch marker up as you progress.

apple

A rosy red apple should make
Grandma feel better—as long
as the wolf doesn't eat it first.

you will need

Yarn
Bulky (Chunky) weight:
Small quantities of (**A**) Red,
(**B**) Brown, and (**C**) Green

Hooks & Notions
US 8/H (5mm) crochet hook
Removable stitch marker
Small amount of toy stuffing
Tapestry needle

Gauge
Gauge is not critical but adjust
your hook to produce a firm fabric.

Size
One size:
2¾in (7cm) high x 7¾in (19.5cm)
circumference

Abbreviations
See page 8.

for the apple

Round 1: Using A, leaving a long tail, make a magic ring
and ss to secure. Work 6sc into ring, pm. (6 sts)
Working in spirals, moving the marker up as you work,
continue as follows:

Round 2: 2sc in each st around. (12 sts)

Round 3: *2sc in next st, 1sc in next st; rep from * around.
(18 sts)

Round 4: *2sc in next st, 1sc in next
2 sts; rep from * around. (24 sts)

Round 5: *2sc in next st, 1sc in next
3 sts; rep from * around. (30 sts)

Rounds 6–11: 1sc in each st around.

Round 12: Sc2tog, 1sc in next 28 sts. (29 sts)

Round 13: 1sc in next 14 sts, sc2tog, 1sc in next 13 sts.
(28 sts)

Round 14: 1sc in next 6 sts, sc2tog,
1sc in next 20 sts. (27 sts)

Round 15: 1sc in next 18 sts,
sc2tog, 1sc in next 7 sts.
(26 sts)

Round 16: Sc2tog, 1sc
in next 24 sts. (25 sts)
Do not fasten off.

pattern notes
Use the stitch marker
tomindicate start of rounds
when working in spirals,
moving the stitch marker
up as you progress.

Pull tail from magic ring through and out of the bottom, gently stuff the apple taking care not to overfill it. Ensure the tail is still poking out of the bottom and continue as follows:

Round 17: *Sc2tog, 1sc in next 2 sts; rep from * to last st, 1sc. (19 sts)

Round 18: *Sc2tog, 1sc in next st; rep from * to last 4 sts, [sc2tog] twice. (12 sts)

Round 19: [Sc2tog] six times, ss in first sc to join.
Fasten off, leaving a long tail.

Make sure the magic ring tail is still poking through the bottom center, then pull and tightly tie it together with the slip stitch tail to give the apple a lovely appley shape.

Weave in all loose ends.

for the stalk

Using B and leaving a long tail, make 6ch, ss in second ch from hook, ss in next 4 sts.
Fasten off, leaving a long tail.

for the leaf

Using C and leaving a long tail, make 7ch, 1sc in second ch from hook, 1hdc in next ch, 1dc in next ch, 1hdc in next ch, 1sc in next ch, ss in next ch. Rotate fabric, and work down the other side of the chain as follows: ss in first ch, 1sc in next ch, 1hdc in next ch, 1dc in next ch, 1hdc in next ch, 1sc in next ch, ss in last ch.
Fasten off, leaving a long tail.

finishing

Using the tapestry needle, thread the long tails of the stalk and the leaf down from the top of the apple, through the center, and out of the bottom. Tie together in a knot and then pull the threads back in and out of the apple at the side to weave in and trim.

pussy cat

HAT WITH CAT EARS • WHITE-TIPPED TAIL

This may sound a little macabre, but our cat is a little black and white sweetie called Treacle. A while ago she vanished for a few days, and while she turned up safely, her tail had gone missing. The big beast was a little upset by this and asked if we could get her a new one, so to placate him, I made one and told him that if Treacle wanted to, she could wear this one. Big beast was happy (and don't worry, Treacle is perfectly alright) and then small beast, who is very attached to the cat, asked if he could wear it. The mask then seemed the natural accompaniment.

complete the look

A simple black top with either leggings or tights is all you need to go with this. A really cute finishing touch would be to wear one white sock and one black sock to have little mismatched paws.

hat with cat ears

This is such an easy costume to put on and purr about, it gets played with a lot.

you will need

Yarn

Bulky (Chunky) weight:
1¾oz (50g) of Black

Hooks & Notions

US I/9 (5.5mm) crochet hook
Tapestry needle

Gauge

Gauge is not critical but adjust the hook size to produce a firm fabric.

Size

One size: To fit 4–7 years
18½in (47cm) circumference

Abbreviations

See page 8.

for the hat

Round 1: Using A, make a magic ring, secure with ss. 3ch (counts as 1dc now and throughout), work 11dc into ring, ss in third ch of t-ch to join. (12 sts)

Round 2: 3ch, 1dc in base of ch, 2dc in each st around, ss in third ch of t-ch to join. (24 sts)

Round 3: 3ch, 1dc in base of ch, 1dc in next st, *2dc in next st, 1dc in next st; rep from * around, ss in third ch of t-ch to join. (36 sts)

Round 4: 1ch, 1dc in base of ch, 1dc in next 2 sts, *2dc in next st, 1dc in next 2 sts; rep from * around, ss in third ch of t-ch to join. (48 sts)

Rounds 5–12: 3ch, 1dc in each st around, ss in third ch of t-ch to join.

Round 13 (eyehole round): 3ch, 1dc in next 10 sts, 1tr in next st, 1dtr in next st, 10ch, miss 6 sts, 1dtr in next 3 sts, 10ch, miss 6 sts, 1dtr in next st, 1tr in next st, 1dc in each st to end, ss in third ch of t-ch to join. (36 sts and two sets of 10ch-sp)

Round 14: 3ch, 1dc in each st to eyeholes, 8dc around the whole chain (rather than through the sts), 1dc in each st between the eyes, 8dc around second eyehole chain, 1dc in each of next 5 sts, dc2tog, 1dc in next 5 sts, dc2tog, 1dc in next 5 sts, dc2tog, ss in third ch of t-ch to join. Fasten off.

for the ears (make 2)

Make 8ch, ss in second ch from hook, 1sc in next ch, 1hdc in next ch, 1tr in next ch, 1dtr in next ch, 3ch, ss in end of ch. Working along the other side of the foundation chain, 3ch, 1dtr in next ch, 1tr in next ch, 1dc in next ch, 1hdc in next ch, 1sc in next ch, ss in last ch. Fasten off leaving a long tail.

finishing

Attach ears in desired position. Weave in all loose ends (see page 124).

pattern notes

Adjust the size to fit 2–3 years by omitting Round 4.

To make the hat in a larger size, use a US K/10½ (7mm) crochet hook, and omit Round 4.

white-tipped tail

This black-and-white tail can be swished about
in all sorts of ways.

you will need

Yarn
Bulky (Chunky) weight yarn:
1oz (25g) of (**A**) Black
Small quantity of (**B**) White

Hooks & Notions
US I/9 (5.5mm) crochet hook
Removable stitch marker
Toy stuffing
Length of black ribbon
Matching sewing needle
and thread
Tapestry needle

Gauge
Gauge is not critical but
adjust the hook size to
produce a firm fabric.

Size
One size: 13in (33cm) long

Abbreviations
See page 8.

for the tail

Note: You will find it easiest to
stuff the tail as you go by adding
the stuffing every ten rounds.
Round 1: Using A, make a magic ring
and secure with ss. Work 8sc into
ring, ss in first sc to join, 1ch, pm.
(8 sts)
Work in spirals as follows, moving
the stitch marker up each round:
Rounds 2–42: 1sc in each st around.
(8 sts)
Fasten off A, join B, and continue
in spirals as follows:
Rounds 43–47: 1sc in each st
around.
Round 48: [Sc2tog] four times,
ensuring the stuffing is right
to the end of the tail.
Fasten off and close
the opening.
Weave in all loose ends
(see page 124).

finishing

Sew the black end of the tail
securely to the mid-point of the
ribbon and use for tying around
the waist of your little kitten.

magic unicorn

HORN HEADDRESS · SWISHY TAIL

I have an identical twin—yep, a proper one, and we have a lot of fun confusing the neighbors and children! This pattern is one that she begged me to make for her. I was reticent because let's face it, it's never going to be the easiest thing to make, but actually it came together really quickly, and there is something extremely pleasing about seeing a grown woman clapping her hands like a five-year-old when presented with something you've made.

horn headdress

Use any color you like for the mane and tail. I used two shades of pink, but you could equally make them in gray or white for a more sophisticated unicorn.

pattern notes

Adjust the size to fit age 2–3 years by omitting Round 4.

you will need

Yarn

Bulky (Chunky) weight: 1¾oz (50g) of (**A**) White

Light Worsted (DK) weight: 1oz (25g) each of (**B**) White, (**C**) Pale Pink, and (**D**) Neon Pink

Metallic Fingering (4ply) weight: Small quantity of (**E**) White or Silver

Note: If you can't find a metallic yarn, substitute it with an alternative Fingering (4ply) weight yarn in a suitable color.

Hooks & Notions

US G/6 (4mm) crochet hook
US I/9 (5.5mm) crochet hook
Removable stitch marker
Small amount of toy stuffing
Tapestry needle

Gauge

Gauge is not critical but adjust the hook size to produce a firm fabric.

Size

One size: To fit 4–7 years
18½in (47cm) circumference

Abbreviations

See page 8.

for the hat

Round 1: Using A and US I/9 (5.5mm) hook, make a magic ring and secure with ss. 3ch (counts as 1dc now and throughout), work 11dc into ring, ss in third ch of t-ch to join. (12 sts)

Round 2: 3ch, 1dc in base of ch, 2dc in each st around, ss in third ch of t-ch to join. (24 sts)

Round 3: 3ch, 1dc at base of ch, 1dc in next st, *2dc in next st, 1dc in next st; rep from * to end, ss in third ch of t-ch to join. (36 sts)

Round 4: 3ch, 1dc at base of ch, 1dc in next 2 sts, *2dc in next st, 1dc in next 2 sts; rep from * to end, ss in third ch of t-ch to join. (48 sts)

Rounds 5–12: 3ch, 1dc in each st around, ss in third ch of t-ch to join. Continue as follows to make the chin-strap: *Make 62ch, 1dc in fourth ch from hook, 1dc in each ch back to the hat, ss in next 2 sts. Fasten off. Count 22 sts along, rejoin yarn, and rep from * once more.

for the horn

Using B and E held together and US G/6 (4mm) hook, 3ch, ss in first ch to make a ring.

Working in spirals and using a stitch marker to indicate beginning of the round, continue as follows:

Round 1: 4sc into the ring. (4 sts)

Round 2: 2sc in first st, 1sc in next 3 sts. (5 sts)

Round 3: 1sc in next 2 sts, 2sc in next st, 1sc in next 2 sts. (6 sts)

Round 4: 2sc in first st, 1sc in next 5 sts. (7 sts)

Round 5: 1sc in next 3 sts, 2sc in next st, 1sc in next 3 sts. (8 sts)

Round 6: 2sc in first st, 1sc in next 7 sts. (9 sts)

Round 7: 1sc in next 4 sts, 2sc in next st, 1sc in next 4 sts. (10 sts)

Round 8: 2sc in first st, 1sc in next 9 sts. (11 sts)

Round 9: 1sc in next 5 sts, 2sc in next st, 1sc in next 5 sts. (12 sts)

Round 10: 2sc in first st, 1sc in next 11 sts. (13 sts)

Round 11: 1sc in next 6 sts, 2sc in next st, 1sc in next 6 sts. (14 sts)

Round 12: 2sc in first st, 1sc in next 13 sts. (15 sts)

Round 13: 1sc in next 7 sts, 2sc in next st, 1sc in next 7 sts. (16 sts)

Round 14: 2sc in first st, 1sc in next 15 sts, ss in first sc to join. (17 sts) Fasten off.

for the mane

Using C and D held together and US I/9 (5.5mm) hook, join yarn at middle point of the back of the hat edge. **Make 60ch, 1sc in second ch from hook, 1sc in each ch back to the hat, ss into hat one row above where you started**. Following a line up the center of the hat, 1sc in next row up and rep from ** to ** a further 8 times.

Work a further six lengths of mane repeating from ** to ** but reducing the number of starting chains by 5 each time. So for the next length make 55ch, the following make 50ch, and so on, finishing with a 35ch length.
Fasten off.

finishing

Stuff the horn and sew to the center front of the hat.
Weave in all ends (see page 124).

swishy tail

For a thicker tail, just crochet more strands until you run out of yarn.

you will need

Yarn
Light Worsted (DK) weight: Small quantity of (**A**) Pale Pink and (**B**) Neon Pink

Hooks & Notions
US I/9 (5.5mm) crochet hook
Length of ribbon
Matching sewing needle and thread
Tapestry needle

Gauge
Gauge is not critical but adjust your hook to produce a flexible fabric.

Size
One size: 12in (30.5cm) long

Abbreviations
See page 8.

for the tail

Using A and B held together, *make 60ch, 1sc in second ch from hook, 1sc in each ch to end; rep from * twice more.
Fasten off.

finishing

Stitch the tail securely to the mid-point of the ribbon and use for tying around the waist of your little unicorn.

vigo the viking

HELMET • THOR'S HAMMER • VIKING CUFFS

One of my (many!) nephews is an utter sweetheart whose middle name is Thor. This costume collection was made purely for him, although the hammer has been pinched and used by all the family for general Thor-like purposes. The helmet sits up nice and high off the head, just to give it that extra Viking look.

complete the look

We made a really simple tabard to go with this outfit by cutting a hole for the head in the center of a long rectangle of fabric. Pop a belt around it and ta-dah! You could just as easily use a big old t-shirt instead.

helmet

If you want to ward off blows from battle-axes and boulders, you need a stout Viking helmet to protect you.

you will need

Yarn

Bulky (Chunky) weight:
3¹⁄₂oz (100g) of Gray (**A**)
Small quantity of White (**B**)

Hooks & Notions

US K/10¹⁄₂ (7mm) crochet hook
Removable stitch marker
Small amount of toy stuffing
Tapestry needle

Gauge

Gauge is not critical but adjust the hook size to produce a firm fabric.

Size

One size: To fit 4–7 years
18in (45.5cm) circumference

Abbreviations

See page 8.

for the helmet

Round 1: Using A, make a magic ring, secure with ss. Work 6sc into ring, ss in first sc to join, 1ch, pm. (6 sts)

Working in spirals, moving the marker up as you work, continue as follows:

Round 2: 2dc in each st around. (12 sts)

Round 3: *2dc in next st, 1dc in next st; rep from * a further five times. (18 sts)

Round 4: *2dc in next st, 1dc in next 2 sts; rep from * a further five times. (24 sts)

Round 5: *2dc in next st, 1dc in next 3 sts; rep from * a further five times. (30 sts)

Round 6: *2dc in next st, 1dc in next 4 sts; rep from * a further five times. (36 sts)

Rounds 7–16: 1dc in each st around.

Round 17: 1dc in each st around, ss in first dc to join.
Fasten off.

pattern notes

For a metallic effect, hold a strand of thin sparkly thread together with the gray as you work.

for the horns (make 2)

Using B, make 14ch, ss in first ch to make a loop.

Rounds 1–3: 1ch, 1sc in each st around.

Rounds 4–5: 1ch, [sc2tog] twice, 1sc in next 4 sts, 2sc in each of next 2 sts, 1sc in next 4 sts, ss in first sc to join. (14 sts)

Round 6: 1ch, [sc2tog] three times, 1sc in next 2 sts st, [sc2tog] twice, 1sc in last 2 sts, ss in first sc to join. (9 sts)

Round 7: 1ch, [sc2tog] four times, 1sc in last st, ss in first sc to join. (5 sts)

Round 8: 1ch, [sc2tog] twice, 1sc in last st, ss in first sc to join. (2 sts)

Round 9: Sc2tog to close.

Fasten off, leaving a long tail that you can use to attach the horn to the hat.

Fill with toy stuffing through the open end.

finishing

Attach the horns to the helmet approximately 2in (5cm) from the bottom of the helmet on either side using the long tails.

Weave in all loose ends (see page 124).

Thor's hammer

This hammer is one of the most played with objects in our house, whether it's for being Thor, or just bashing each other!

you will need

Yarn

Bulky (Chunky) weight: 3½oz (100g) of (**A**) Grey Small quantity of (**B**) Light Brown, and (**C**) Dark Brown

Hooks & Notions

US H/8 (5mm) crochet hook
Small amount of toy stuffing
Removable stitch marker
Tapestry needle

Gauge

Gauge is not critical but adjust the hook size to produce a firm fabric.

Size

One size: 10in (25cm) from base of handle to top of hammer

Abbreviations

See page 8.

for the hammerhead

Using A, make 22ch.
Rows 1–6: 1dc in third ch from hook, 1dc in each ch to end, turn. (20 sts)
Row 7: 3ch (counts as 1dc now and throughout), working in front loop only 1dc in each st to end, turn.
Rows 8–10: 3ch, 1dc in each st to end, turn.
Row 11: Repeat Row 7.
Rows 12–16: Repeat Row 8.
Rows 17–20: Repeat Rows 7–10.
Fasten off, leaving a long tail.
Use the tail to sew the long edges together.

for the end panels [make 2]

Using A, make 12ch.
Row 1: 1dc in third ch from hook and in each ch to end, turn. (10 sts)
Rows 2–6: 3ch (counts as a st now and throughout), 1dc in next 9 sts, turn. (10 sts)
Fasten off, leaving a long tail. Use the long tails to sew the end panels at either end and fill with toy stuffing before closing the second end panel.

for the handle

Round 1: Using B and C held together, make a magic ring, secure with ss. Work 8sc into ring, ss in first sc to join, 1ch, pm. (8 sts)
Working in spirals, moving the marker up as you work, continue as follows:
Rounds 2–23: 1dc in each st around.
Ss in last dc to join and fasten off, leaving a long tail.

finishing

Firmly stuff the handle and use the tail to attach the handle to the head.
Weave in all loose ends (see page 124).

pattern notes

For a metallic effect, hold a strand of thin sparkly thread together with the gray as you work.

viking cuffs

These are made in brown yarn to look like the leather cuffs worn by real Viking warriors to protect them in sword fights.

you will need

Yarn

Light Worsted (DK) weight:
1¾oz (50g) of (**A**) Brown
Small amount of (**B**) Gray

Hooks & Notions

US H/8 (5mm) crochet hook
Tapestry needle

Gauge

Gauge is not critical but the fabric should be firm yet flexible.

Size

One size: To fit 4–7 years
6½in (16.5cm) circumference

Abbreviations

See page 8.

for the cuffs (make 2)

Using A, make 26ch.
Row 1: 1sc in second ch from hook, 1sc in each ch to end, turn. (25 sts)
Rows 2–5: 1ch, 1sc in each st to end, turn.
Fasten off, leaving a long tail.

finishing

Using the long tails, sew the short edges together. With B (and following the photographs for guidance), embroider three large crossed stitches into the cuff.

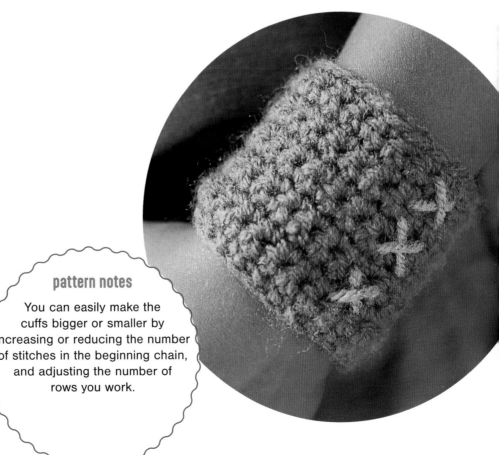

pattern notes

You can easily make the cuffs bigger or smaller by increasing or reducing the number of stitches in the beginning chain, and adjusting the number of rows you work.

rapunzel

BRAIDED HAIR · SHRUG

I have to confess that this was actually made just to please me, although it has proved extremely popular with all the little girls who come round to play! The chunky construction means it will stay looking lovely through many dress-up sessions. This really is one of those patterns that I wish I'd had when I was a little girl, because I honestly would have worn it until it fell apart! The shrug is one of the first things I learned to make and is so simple it's ridiculous! In fact, I have three of these that I wear on rotation all summer.

complete the look

A simple cotton summer dress is all you need for this, but if your Rapunzel happens to have a ball gown, then why not!

braided hair

The head part and the braid of Rapunzel's wig are made in one continuous piece of crochet.

you will need

Yarn

Bulky (Chunky) weight :
1¾oz (50g) of (**A**) Bright Yellow, (**B**) Lemon Yellow, and (**C**) White

Hooks & Notions

US L/11 (8mm) crochet hook
Tapestry needle

Gauge

Gauge is not critical but adjust the hook size to produce a firm fabric.

Size

One size: To fit 4–7 years
18½in (47cm) circumference

Abbreviations

See page 8.

for the head

Round 1: Using A, B, and C held together, make a magic ring and secure with ss. 3ch (counts as 1dc now and throughout), 5dc into ring, ss in third ch of t-ch to join. (6 sts)

Round 2: 3ch, 1dc in base of ch, 2dc in each st to end, ss in third ch of t-ch to join. (12 sts)

Round 3: 3ch, 1dc in base of ch, 1dc in next st, *2dc in next st, 1dc in next st; rep from * a further four times, ss in third ch of t-ch to join. (18 sts)

Round 4: 3ch, 1dc in base of ch, 1dc in next 2 sts, *2dc in next st, 1dc in next 2 sts; rep from * a further four times, ss in third ch of t-ch to join. (24 sts)

Round 5: 3ch, 1dc in base of ch, 1dc in next 3 sts, *2dc in next st, 1dc in next 3 sts; rep from * a further four times, ss in third ch of t-ch to join. (30 sts)

Round 6: 3ch, 1dc in base of ch, 1dc in next 4 sts, *2dc in next st, 1dc in next 4 sts; rep from * a further four times, ss in third ch of t-ch to join. (36 sts)

Rounds 7–10: 3ch, 1dc in each st around, ss in third ch of t-ch to join.

for the hair

**Using A, B, and C held together, make 92ch, 1dc in fourth ch from hook, 1dc in each ch, miss 2 sts on edge of hat, ss in next st to attach; rep from ** twice more.
Fasten off.
Working back and forth (without turning your work), create the hairline as follows:

Row 1: Rejoin yarn 10 sts from where the hair was fastened off. Make 16ch, miss 9 sts to the left, ss in next st of brim.

Row 2: 14ch, miss 8 sts to the right (next to where you started the fringe), ss in brim.

Row 3: 12ch, miss 7 sts to the right, ss in brim.

Row 4: 10ch, miss 6 sts to the left, ss in brim.

Row 5: 8ch, miss 5 sts to the right, ss in brim.

Row 6: 6ch, miss 4 sts to the left, ss in brim. Fasten off.

Rejoin yarn where you originally started the hairline and work as follows:

Row 1: 8ch, miss 4 sts to the left, ss in brim.

Row 2: 6ch, miss 4 sts to the left, ss in brim.

Row 3: 5ch, miss 3 sts to the right, ss in brim. Fasten off.

finishing

Weave in all loose ends (see page 124). Braid the three hair strands and secure with a few stitches to keep them braided together. Add flowers as desired—see pattern notes for details.

shrug

A pretty pink shrug completes Rapunzel's costume, but would work just as well with any princess outfit.

you will need

Yarn

Light Worsted (DK) weight: 1³⁄₄oz (50g) of Pink

Hooks & Notions

US G/6 (4mm) crochet hook
Tapestry needle

Gauge

Gauge is not critical but the fabric should be flexible.

Size

One size: To fit 4–7 years
20 x 9in (51 x 23cm)
before seaming

Abbreviations

See page 8.

for the shrug

Row 1 (RS): Make 73ch, work 2dc in fifth ch from hook, 1ch, 2dc in next ch, *miss 3 ch, 2dc in next ch, 1ch, 2dc in next ch; rep from * to last 2 ch, miss 1 ch, 1dc in last ch, turn.

Row 2: 3ch, miss 2 sts, [2dc, 1ch, 2dc] in 1ch-sp from previous row, *miss 4 sts, [2dc, ch 1, 2dc] in 1ch-sp from previous row; rep from * to last 2 sts, miss 2 sts, 1dc in third ch of t-ch, turn.

Rows 3–19: Repeat Row 2.

Fasten off.

finishing

Weave in loose ends and gently block the rectangle according to the ball band instructions (see page 124).

Lay the piece flat with right side of fabric facing. Fold in half, so the longer edges meet and the wrong side is now facing you. Working from the outside in (along the long edge), seam approximately 1in (2.5cm) on the right-hand side to create an armhole.

Repeat for the other side.

Fasten off. Weave in all ends.

wicked witch

BLACK HAT • COBWEB COLLAR • SPIDER

complete the look

Well, really, you should have hobnail boots, a cape made of the night sky, and a dress woven from pure darkness, but if you don't have those around the house then some striped tights and old black clothes will do nicely!

Having made the snowflake collar for the Snow Queen outfit (see page 42), the next thing to pop into my head was a cobweb collar, so this costume actually started at the neck and worked its way up to the hat. The geek in me wanted a perfect cone for the hat, so while there are other more traditional ways to crochet a cone, this one takes a little more concentration but the outcome is really good and worth the extra effort.

black hat

Every witch needs a hat, under which she can hide frogs, newts, and anything else she needs to keep handy for her cauldron.

pattern notes

The rounds of treble crochet toward the base of the hat provide a bit more stretch, making the hat comfier and more secure to wear.

you will need

Yarn
Bulky (Chunky) weight:
3½oz (100g) of Black

Hooks & Notions
US I/9 (5.5mm) crochet hook
Removable stitch marker
Tapestry needle

Gauge
Gauge is not critical but adjust the hook size to produce a firm fabric.

Size
One size: To fit 4–7 years
19½in (50cm) circumference (excluding brim); 11½in (29cm) tall

Abbreviations
See page 8.

for the hat

Make 3ch, ss in first ch to make a ring.
Working in spirals, moving the marker up as you work, continue as follows:
Round 1: 4sc into the ring, pm. (4 sts)
Round 2: *2sc in next st, 1sc in next st; rep from * around. (6 sts)
Round 3: *2sc in next st, 1sc in next 2 sts; rep from * around. (8 sts)
Round 4: 1sc in next 2 sts, 2sc in next st, 1sc in next 3 sts, 2sc in next st, 1sc in next st. (10 sts)
Round 5: 1sc in next st, 2sc in next st, 1sc in next 4 sts, 2sc in next st, 1sc in next 3 sts. (12 sts)
Round 6: 1sc in next 4 sts, 2sc in next st, 1sc in next 5 sts, 2sc in next st, 1sc in next st. (14 sts)
Round 7: 2sc in next st, 1sc in next 6 sts, 2sc in next st, 1sc in next 6 sts. (16 sts)
Round 8: 1sc in next 4 sts, 2sc in next st, 1sc in next 7 sts, 2sc in next st, 1sc in next 3 sts. (18 sts)
Round 9: 1sc in next 8 sts, 2sc in next st, 1sc in next 8 sts, 2sc in next st. (20 sts)
Round 10: 1sc in next 2 sts, 2sc in next st, 1sc in next 9 sts, 2sc in next st, 1sc in next 7 sts. (22 sts)
Round 11: 1sc in next 6 sts, 2sc in next st, 1sc in next 10 sts, 2sc in next st, 1sc in next 4 sts. (24 sts)
Round 12: 2sc in next st, 1sc in next 11 sts, 2sc in next st, 1sc in next 11 sts. (26 sts)
Round 13: 1sc in next 5 sts, 2sc in next st, 1sc in next 12 sts, 2sc in next st, 1sc in next 7 sts. (28 sts)
Round 14: 1sc in next 11 sts, 2sc in next st, 1sc in next 13 sts, 2sc in next st, 1sc in next 2 sts. (30 sts)
Round 15: 1sc in next 4 sts, 2sc in next st, 1sc in next 14 sts, 2sc in next st, 1sc in next 10 sts. (32 sts)

Round 16: 2sc in next st, 1sc in next 15 sts, 2sc in next st, 1sc in next 15 sts. (34 sts)

Round 17: 1sc in next 10 sts, 2sc in next st, 1sc in next 16 sts, 2sc in next st, 1sc in next 6 sts. (36 sts)

Round 18: 1sc in next 3 sts, 2sc in next st, 1sc in next 17 sts, 2sc in next st, 1sc in next 14 sts. (38 sts)

Round 19: 1sc in next 15 sts, 2sc in next st, 1sc in next 18 sts, 2sc in next st, 1sc in next 14 sts. (40 sts)

Round 20: 1sc in next 9 sts, 2sc in next st, 1sc in next 19 sts, 2sc in next st, 1sc in next 10 sts. (42 sts)

Round 21: 1sc in next st, 2sc in next st, 1sc in next 20 sts, 2sc in next st, 1sc in next 19 sts. (44 sts)

Round 22: 1sc in next 16 sts, 2sc in next st, 1sc in next 21 sts, 2sc in next st, 1sc in next 5 sts. (46 sts)

Round 23: 1sc in next 8 sts, 2sc in next st, 1sc in next 22 sts, 2sc in next st, 1sc in next 14 sts. (48 sts)

Round 24: 1sc in next 23 sts, 2sc in next st, 1sc in next 23 sts, 2sc in next st. (50 sts)

Round 25: 1sc in next 16 sts, 2sc in next st, 1sc in next 24 sts, 2sc in next st, 1sc in next 8 sts. (52 sts)

Round 26: 1sc in next 8 sts, 2sc in next st, 1sc in next 25 sts, 2sc in next st, 1sc in next 17 sts. (54 sts)

Round 27: 2sc in next st, 1sc in next 26 sts, 2sc in next st, 1sc in next 26 sts. (56 sts)

Round 28: 1sc in next 17 sts, 2sc in next st, 1sc in next 27 sts, 2sc in next st, 1sc in next 10 sts. (58 sts)

Round 29: 1sc in next 7 sts, 2sc in next st, 1sc in next 28 sts, 2sc in next st, 1sc in next 21 sts. (60 sts)
Working in rounds, continue as follows:

Rounds 30–34: 3ch (counts as 1dc), 1dc in each st around.

Working in spirals again, continue as follows for the brim:

Round 35: For this round only, work into the front loop of each st as follows: *1sc in next 9 sts, 2sc in next st; rep from * a further five times. (66 sts)

Round 36: *1sc in next 10 sts, 2sc in next st; rep from * a further five times. (72 sts)

Round 37: *1sc in next 11 sts, 2sc in next st; rep from * a further five times. (78 sts)

Round 38: *1sc in next 12 sts, 2sc in next st; rep from * a further five times. (84 sts)

Round 39: *1sc in next 13 sts, 2sc in next st; rep from * a further five times. (90 sts)

Round 40: *1sc in next 14 sts, 2sc in next st; rep from * a further five times. (96 sts)
Fasten off.

finishing

Weave in all loose ends (see page 124) and let the brim curl up slightly.
Stand back and admire the beautiful cone!

cobweb collar

This cute little collar would look just as good on an adult, as part of a Halloween costume.

you will need

Yarn

Light Worsted (DK) weight:
Small quantity of Black

Hooks & Notions

US G/6 (4mm) crochet hook
30in (75cm) black ribbon
Tapestry needle

Gauge

Gauge is not critical but adjust
your hook to produce a firm fabric.

Size

One size: 15in (37.5cm) wide
(excluding ribbon)

Abbreviations

See page 8.

for the cobweb motif (make 5)

Round 1: Make a magic ring and secure with ss. Work 5sc into ring, ss in first sc to join, pm. (5 sts)

Round 2: *Make 11ch, ss in second ch from hook and each ch back to sc, ss in next st; rep from * a further four times. Five "spokes" created. Fasten off.

Round 3: Starting from the center circle, count up 2 sts on one of your previous 11ch spokes, rejoin yarn, *3ch, and then ss into second stitch up of the next 11ch spoke; rep from * a further four times.

Round 4: Starting from the center circle, count up 6 sts on one of your previous 11ch spokes, rejoin yarn, *6ch, and then ss into sixth st up of your next 11ch spoke; rep from * a further four times.
Fasten off.

Round 5: Starting from the center circle, count up 8 sts on one of your previous 11ch spokes, rejoin yarn, *11ch, and then ss into eighth st up of your next 11ch spoke; rep from * a further four times.
Fasten off leaving a long tail.

finishing

Lay the five motifs out so one side from each is touching the next one and sew them together.
Weave in all loose ends (see page 124).
Thread the ribbon through either side of the cobweb panel and tie in a bow around your witch's neck.

pattern notes

Adjust the size of the collar by adding more or fewer cobwebs and altering the length of the ribbon.

Hold a strand of silver metallic embroidery floss together with the yarn as you work to make sparkly cobwebs.

spider

**An amigurumi spider completes the costume—
a vital ingredient for casting spells.**

you will need

Yarn

Light Worsted (DK) weight:
Small quantity of Black

Hooks & Notions

US G/6 (4mm) crochet hook
Removable stitch marker
Toy stuffing
Silver embroidery floss
Embroidery needle
Tapestry needle

Gauge

Gauge is not critical but adjust the
hook size to produce a firm fabric.

Size

One size: 1¼in (3cm)
excluding legs

Abbreviations

See page 8.

for the body

Round 1: Make a magic ring and secure with ss. Work 6sc
into ring, ss in first sc to join, pm. (6 sts)
Working in spirals and using a stitch marker to indicate
beginning of the round, continue as follows:
Round 2: 2sc in each st around. (12 sts)
Round 3: *2sc in next st, 1sc in next st; rep from * a further
five times. (18 sts)
Round 4: 1sc in each st around.
Round 5: *Sc2tog, 1sc in next st; rep from * a further
five times. (12 sts)
Stuff the spider and continue as follows:
Round 5: *Sc2tog; rep from * a further five times. (6 sts)
Fasten off and close the end.

for the legs (make 8)

Make 8ch.
Fasten off, leaving a long tail.

finishing

Sew the legs to the body. Weave in all loose ends (see
page 124).
Use the silver embroidery floss to stitch a little face on
and pull the thread up through the top of his body to make
a long thread to dangle it from. He can either be attached
to the tip or brim of the hat, hung from the collar, or just
be sat on a shoulder to give people a fright!

wily wizard

STARRY HAT • BEARD

There's a funny old book from the 1970s called *Melric the Magician Who Lost His Magic,* which my eldest son loves! Melric wears a red and yellow hat, in fact his whole outfit is red with yellow stars, and so a red and yellow wizard hat was requested for wearing to World Book Day at school. Abracadabra! My son came home with the "best costume" prize—I think I was probably more excited than he was!

complete the look

You could just wear an oversized t-shirt with a belt around the middle and jogging bottoms, or an old dressing gown, but if you want to go all out and create a real showstopper, embellish the clothing with printed stars. Cut a potato in half and carve a star shape into it. Using fabric paint, let the kids go wild stamping stars on to the t-shirt or dressing gown. Leave the garment to dry thoroughly and ta-dah!

starry hat

Abracadabra! You could make this hat up in any color you like, but red is our favorite.

you will need

Yarn

Bulky (Chunky) weight:
2¾oz (75g) of (**A**) Red

Light Worsted (DK) weight:
Small quantity of (**B**) Yellow

Hooks & Notions

US I/9 (5.5mm) crochet hook
US G/6 (4mm) crochet hook
Removable stitch marker
Tapestry needle

Gauge

Gauge is not critical but adjust the hook size to produce a firm fabric.

Size

One Size: To fit 4–7 years
19½in (48cm) circumference;
15½in (39.5cm) tall

Abbreviations

See page 8.

for the hat

Using A and US I/9 (5.5mm) hook, make 3ch, ss in first ch to make a ring.

Working in spirals and, using a stitch marker to indicate beginning of the round, continue as follows:

Round 1: 4sc into the ring. (4 sts)

Round 2: 2sc in first st, 1sc in next 3 sts. (5 sts)

Round 3: 1sc in next 2 sts, 2sc in next st, 1sc in next 2 sts. (6 sts)

Round 4: 2sc in first st, 1sc in next 5 sts. (7 sts)

Round 5: 1sc in next 3 sts, 2sc in next st, 1sc in next 3 sts. (8 sts)

Round 6: 2sc in first st, 1sc in next 7 sts. (9 sts)

Round 7: 1sc in next 4 sts, 2sc in next st, 1sc in next 4 sts. (10 sts)

Round 8: 2sc in first st, 1sc in next 9 sts. (11 sts)

Round 9: 1sc in next 5 sts, 2sc in next st, 1sc in next 5 sts. (12 sts)

Round 10: 2sc in first st, 1sc in next 11 sts. (13 sts)

Round 11: 1sc in next 6 sts, 2sc in next st, 1sc in next 6 sts. (14 sts)

Round 12: 2sc in first st, 1sc in next 13 sts. (15 sts)

Round 13: 1sc in next 7 sts, 2sc in next st, 1sc in next 7 sts. (16 sts)

Round 14: 2sc in first st, 1sc in next 15 sts. (17 sts)

Round 15: 1sc in next 8 sts, 2sc in next st, 1sc in next 8 sts. (18 sts)

Round 16: 2sc in first st, 1sc in next 17 sts. (19 sts)

Round 17: 1sc in next 9 sts, 2sc in next st, 1sc in next 9 sts. (20 sts)

Round 18: 2sc in first st, 1sc in next 19 sts. (21 sts)

Round 19: 1sc in next 10 sts, 2sc in next st, 1sc in next 10 sts. (22 sts)

Round 20: 2sc in first st, 1sc in next 21 sts. (23 sts)

Round 21: 1sc in next 11 sts, 2sc in next st, 1sc in next 11 sts. (24 sts)

Round 22: 2sc in first st, 1sc in next 23 sts. (25 sts)

Round 23: 1sc in next 12 sts, 2sc in next st, 1sc in next 12 sts. (26 sts)

Round 24: 2sc in first st, 1sc in next 25 sts. (27 sts)

Round 25: 1sc in next 13 sts, 2sc in next st, 1sc in next 13 sts. (28 sts)

Round 26: 2sc in first st, 1sc in next 27 sts. (29 sts)

Round 27: 1sc in next 14 sts, 2sc in next st, 1sc in next 14 sts. (30 sts)

Round 28: 2sc in first st, 1sc in next 29 sts. (31 sts)

Round 29: 1sc in next 15 sts, 2sc in next st, 1sc in next 15 sts. (32 sts)

Round 30: 2sc in first st, 1sc in next 31 sts. (33 sts)

Round 31: 1sc in next 16 sts, 2sc in next st, 1sc in next 16 sts. (34 sts)

Round 32: 2sc in first st, 1sc in next 33 sts. (35 sts)

Round 33: 1sc in next 17 sts, 2sc in next st, 1sc in next 17 sts. (36 sts)

Round 34: 2sc in first st, 1sc in next 35 sts. (37 sts)

Round 35: 1sc in next 18 sts, 2sc in next st, 1sc in next 18 sts. (38 sts)

Round 36: 2sc in first st, 1sc in next 37 sts. (39 sts)

Round 37: 1sc in next 19 sts, 2sc in next st, 1sc in next 19 sts. (40 sts)

Round 38: 2sc in first st, 1sc in next 39 sts. (41 sts)

Round 39: 1sc in next 20 sts, 2sc in next st, 1sc in next 20 sts. (42 sts)

Round 40: 2sc in first st, 1sc in next 41 sts. (43 sts)

Round 41: 1sc in next 21 sts, 2sc in next st, 1sc in next 21 sts. (44 sts)

Round 42: 2sc in first st, 1sc in next 43 sts. (45 sts)

Round 43: 1sc in next 22 sts, 2sc in next st, 1sc in next 22 sts. (46 sts)

Round 44: 2sc in first st, 1sc in next 45 sts. (47 sts)

Round 45: 1sc in next 23 sts, 2sc in next st, 1sc in next 23 sts. (48 sts)

Round 46: 2sc in first st, 1sc in next 47 sts. (49 sts)

Round 47: 1sc in next 24 sts, 2sc in next st, 1sc in next 24 sts. (50 sts)

Round 48: 2sc in first st, 1sc in next 49 sts. (51 sts)

Round 49: 1sc in next 25 sts, 2sc in next st, 1sc in next 25 sts. (52 sts)

Round 50: 2sc in first st, 1sc in next 51 sts. (53 sts)

Round 51: 1sc in next 26 sts, 2sc in next st, 1sc in next 26 sts. (54 sts)

Round 52: 2sc in first st, 1sc in next 53 sts. (55 sts)

Round 53: 1sc in next 27 sts, 2sc in next st, 1sc in next 27 sts, ss in first sc to finish. (56 sts) Fasten off.

for the stars (make 7)

Using B and the US G/6 (4mm) hook, make 3ch, ss in first ch to join.

Round 1: 1ch, 10sc in ring, ss in first sc to join. (10 sts)

Round 2: *5ch, ss in second ch from hook, 1sc in next ch, 1hdc in next ch, 1dc in last ch, miss 1 st, ss in next st; rep from * a further four times. Fasten off, leaving a long tail.

finishing

Using the long tails, stitch the stars onto the hat. Weave in all loose ends (see page 124).

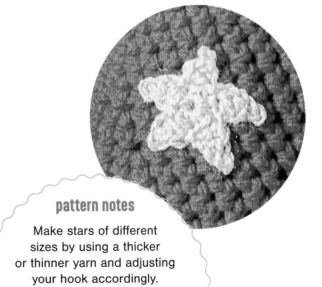

pattern notes

Make stars of different sizes by using a thicker or thinner yarn and adjusting your hook accordingly.

Hold a strand of metallic thread together with the yarn for a sparkly and magical finish.

beard

From Merlin to Melric, a beard is an essential part of the wizard's appearance.

you will need

Yarn

Light Worsted (DK) weight: Small quantity of White

Hooks & Notions

US G/6 (4mm) crochet hook
Tapestry needle

Gauge

Gauge is not critical but adjust the hook size to produce a firm fabric.

Size

One size: To fit 4–7 years
7½in (19cm) wide, 6½in (16.5cm) tall (including mustache)

Abbreviations

See page 8.

for the mustache

Leaving a long tail, make 30ch.
Row 1: Ss in second ch from hook, 1sc in next ch, 1hdc in next 2 ch, 1dc in next 2 ch, 1tr in next 2 ch, 1dtr in next 2 ch, 1tr in next ch, 1dc in next ch, 1hdc in next ch, 1sc in next ch, ss in next ch, 1sc in next ch, 1hdc in next ch, 1dc in next ch, 1tr in next ch, 1dtr in next 2 ch, 1tr in next 2 ch, 1dc in next 2 ch, 1hdc in next 2 ch, 1sc in next ch, ss in last ch to finish.
Fasten off, leaving a long tail.

for the beard

Leaving a long tail, make 22ch.
Row 1: 1dc in fourth ch from hook, 1dc in next 8 ch, 3dc in next ch, 1dc in next 10 ch, turn. (20 sts)
Rows 2–4: 1ch, 1sc in each st to end, turn. (20 sts)
Row 5: 1ch, miss 1 st, 1sc in next 18 sts, miss 1 st, ss in last st, turn. (18 sts)
Row 6: 1ch, miss 1 st, 1sc in next 16 sts, miss 1 st, ss in last st, turn. (16 sts)
Row 7: 1ch, miss 1 st, 1sc in next 14 sts, miss 1 st, ss in last st, turn. (14 sts)

Row 8: 1ch, miss 1 st, 1sc in next 12 sts, miss 1 st, ss in last st, turn. (12 sts)
Rows 9–12: 1ch, 1sc in each st to end, turn. (12 sts)
Row 13: 1ch, miss 1 st, 1sc in next 10 sts, miss 1 st, ss in last st, turn. (10 sts)
Row 14: 1ch, miss 1 st, 1sc in next 8 sts, miss 1 st, ss in last st, turn. (8 sts)
Row 15: 1ch, miss 1 st, 1sc in next 6 sts, miss 1 st, ss in last st, turn. (6 sts)
Row 16: 1ch, miss 1 st, 1sc in next 4 sts, miss 1 st, ss in last st, turn. (4 sts)

finishing

Using the long tails from the beard, sew the corners of the beard to the mustache and tie the long tails on the mustache to make loops to hook over the little wizard's ears.

gray rabbit

HAT WITH RABBIT EARS • WHITE TAIL

My smallest beast isn't a big hat wearer, even when there's snow up to your knees, so this was an attempt to get him into a hat he would be happy with! Any of you out there with stubborn, fashion-conscious creatures will know this was doomed to fail, but what it left us with was a costume to add to the dressing up box that is coveted by the little girl over the road, and worn on a weekly basis.

complete the look

We struggle to find plain tops, so invariably wear an inside-out gray top (usually with some sort of space ship on the outside!) and a pair of tracksuit bottoms. Anything pink or fluffy also works.

hat with rabbit ears

An excellent costume for Easter, this hat and the tail are brought out every March.

you will need

Yarn

Bulky (Chunky) weight:
2¼oz (65g) of (**A**) Light Gray
Small quantities of (**B**) White
and (**C**) Pink

Hooks & Notions

US I/9 (5.5mm) crochet hook
Tapestry needle

Gauge

Gauge is not critical but
adjust the hook size to
produce a firm fabric.

Size

One size: To fit 4–7 years,
18½in (47cm) circumference

Abbreviations

See page 8.

for the hat

Round 1: Using A, make a magic
ring and secure with ss. 3ch (counts
as 1dc now and throughout), work
11dc into ring, ss in third ch of
t-ch to join. (12 sts)

Round 2: 3ch, 1dc in base of ch,
2dc in each st around, ss in third
ch of t-ch to join. (24 sts)

Round 3: 3ch, 1dc at base of ch,
1dc in next st, *2dc in next st, 1dc
in next st; rep from * to end, ss in
third ch of t-ch to join. (36 sts)

Round 4: 3ch, 1dc at base of ch,
1dc in next 2 sts, *2dc in next st,
1dc in next 2 sts; rep from * to end,
ss in third ch of t-ch to join. (48 sts)

Rounds 5–12: 3ch, 1dc in each st
around, ss in third ch of t-ch to join.

Round 13 (eyehole round): 3ch,
1dc in next 13 sts, 1tr in next st, 1dtr
in next st, 10ch, miss 6 sts, 1dtr in
next 2 sts, 10ch, miss 6 sts, 1dtr in
next st, 1tr in next st, 1dc in each st
to end, ss in third ch of t-ch to join.
(36 sts and two sets of 10ch-sp)

Round 14: 3ch, 1dc in next 13 sts,
work 8dc around the chain (rather
than through the sts), 1dc in each
st between the eyes, 8dc around
second chain, 1dc in each of next
10 sts, dc2tog, 2dc. Fasten off A.

Round 15: Join B at any st,
ss around the edge, ss to join.
Fasten off. Weave in ends.

for the rose

Using C, make 3ch.
Work 2dc in third ch from hook.
Fasten off. Sew to the middle
stitches between the eyes as shown.

for the ears (make 2)

Using A, make 16ch, ss in first ch
from hook, 1sc in next ch, 1hdc
in next ch, 1dc in next 10 ch, 3ch,
ss in last ch.
Working along the opposite side
of the foundation ch, continue as
follows: 3ch, miss 1 ch, 1dc in next
10 ch, 1hdc in next ch, 1sc in
next ch, ss in next ch to finish.
Fasten off, leaving a long tail.

pattern notes

Adjust the size to fit
2–3 years by omitting
Round 4.

To make the hat in a larger
size, use a US K/10½ (7mm)
crochet hook and omit
Round 4.

white tail

A little tail puts the finishing touch to the rabbit outfit.

you will need

Yarn

Bulky (Chunky) weight:
1oz (25g) in White

Hooks & Notions

US G/6 (4mm) crochet hook
Removable stitch marker
Small quantity of toy stuffing
Length of matching ribbon
Matching sewing needle
and thread
Tapestry needle

Gauge

Gauge is not critical but adjust the hook size to produce a firm fabric.

Size

One size: 4in (10cm) diameter; 2½in (6cm) high

Abbreviations

See page 8.

for the tail

Round 1: Using A, make a magic ring and secure with ss. Work 6sc into ring, ss in first sc to join, 1ch, pm. (6 sts)
Work in spirals as follows, moving the stitch marker up each round:
Round 2: 2sc in each st around. (12 sts)
Round 3: *2sc in next st, 1sc in next st; rep from * a further five times. (18 sts)
Round 4: *2sc in next st, 1sc in next 2 sts; rep from * a further five times. (24 sts)
Rounds 5–10: 1sc in each st around.
Round 11: *Sc2tog, 1sc in next 2 sts; rep from * a further five times. (18 sts)

Round 12: *Sc2tog, 1sc in next st; rep from * a further five times. (12 sts)
Firmly stuff the tail and continue as follows:
Round 13: [Sc2tog] six times. (6 sts)
Round 14: [Sc2tog] three times, ss in first sc to join. Fasten off.

finishing

Weave in all loose ends (see page 124).
Sew the tail securely at the mid-point of the ribbon and tie the tail in place on your little bunny and watch them hop away!

techniques

In this section, you'll find all the simple crochet and finishing techniques that you'll need to make the projects in this book.

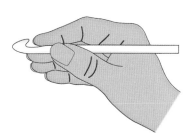

Holding the hook

Pick up your hook as though you are picking up a pen or pencil. Keeping the hook held loosely between your fingers and thumb, turn your hand so that the palm is facing up and the hook is balanced in your hand and resting in the space between your index finger and your thumb.

You can also hold the hook like a knife—this may be easier if you are working with a large hook or with bulky yarn. Choose the method that you find most comfortable.

Holding the yarn

1. Pick up the yarn with your little finger in the opposite hand to your hook, with your palm facing upward and with the short end in front. Turn your hand to face downward, with the yarn on top of your index finger and under the other two fingers and wrapped right around the little finger, as shown above.

2. Turn your hand to face you, ready to hold the work in your middle finger and thumb. Keeping your index finger only at a slight curve, hold the work or the slip knot using the same hand, between your middle finger and your thumb and just below the crochet hook and loop/s on the hook.

Holding the hook and yarn while crocheting

Keep your index finger, with the yarn draped over it, at a slight curve, and hold your work (or the slip knot) using the same hand, between your middle finger and your thumb and just below the crochet hook and loop/s on the hook.

As you draw the loop through the hook release the yarn on the index finger to allow the loop to stay loose on the hook. If you tense your index finger, the yarn will become too tight and pull the loop on the hook too tight for you to draw the yarn through.

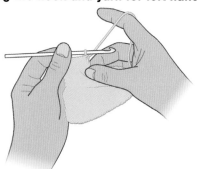

Holding the hook and yarn for left-handers

Some left-handers learn to crochet like right-handers, but others learn with everything reversed—with the hook in the left hand and the yarn in the right.

Making a slip knot

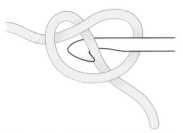

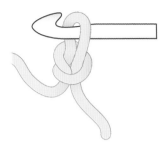

1. In one hand hold the circle at the top where the yarn crosses, and let the tail drop down at the back so that it falls across the center of the loop. With your free hand or the tip of a crochet hook, pull a loop through the circle.

2. Put the hook into the loop and pull gently so that it forms a loose loop on the hook.

Yarn over hook

To create a stitch, catch the yarn from behind with the hook pointing upward. As you gently pull the yarn through the loop on the hook, turn the hook so it faces downward and slide the yarn through the loop. The loop on the hook should be kept loose enough for the hook to slide through easily.

Magic ring

This is a useful starting technique if you do not want a visible hole in the center of your round. Loop the yarn around your finger, insert the hook through the ring, yarn over hook, pull through the ring to make the first chain. Work the number of stitches required into the ring and then pull the end to tighten the center ring and close the hole.

Chain

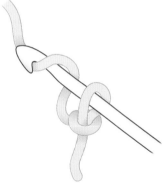

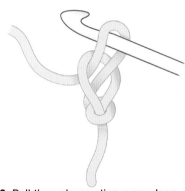

1. Using the hook, wrap the yarn over the hook ready to pull it through the loop on the hook.

2. Pull through, creating a new loop on the hook. Continue in this way to create a chain of the required length.

Chain ring

1. To join the chain into a circle, insert the crochet hook into the first chain that you made (not into the slip knot), yarn over hook.

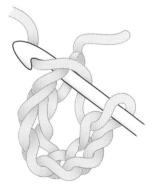

2. Pull the yarn through the chain and through the loop on your hook at the same time, thereby creating a slip stitch and forming a circle. You now have a chain ring ready to work stitches into as instructed in the pattern.

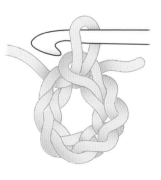

Chain space (ch sp)

1. A chain space is the space that has been made under a chain in the previous round or row, and falls in between other stitches.

2. Stitches into a chain space are made directly into the hole created under the chain and not into the chain stitches themselves.

Slip stitch (ss)

A slip stitch doesn't create any height and is often used as the last stitch to create a smooth and even round or row.

1. A chain space is the space that has been made under a chain in the previous round or row, and falls in between other stitches.

2. Stitches into a chain space are made directly into the hole created under the chain and not into the chain stitches themselves.

Making rounds

When working in rounds the work is not turned, so you are always working from one side. Depending on the pattern you are working, a "round" can be square. Start each round by making one or more chains to create the height you need for the stitch you are working:

Single crochet = 1 chain
Half double crochet = 2 chains
Double crochet = 3 chains
Treble crochet = 4 chains
Double treble crochet = 5 chains

Work the required stitches to complete the round. At the end of the round, slip stitch into the top of the chain to close the round.

Making rows

When making straight rows you turn the work at the end of each row and make a turning chain to create the height you need for the stitch you are working with, as for making rounds.

Single crochet = 1 chain
Half double crochet = 2 chains
Double crochet = 3 chains
Treble crochet = 4 chains
Double treble crochet = 5 chains

Continuous spiral

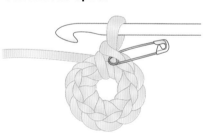

If you work in a spiral you do not need a turning chain. After completing the base ring, place a stitch marker in the first stitch and then continue to crochet around. When you have made a round and reached the point where the stitch marker is, work this stitch, take out the stitch marker from the previous round and put it back into the first stitch of the new round. A safety pin or piece of yarn in a contrasting color makes a good stitch marker.

Working into top of stitch

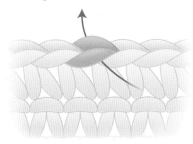

Unless otherwise directed, always insert the hook under both of the two loops on top of the stitch—this is the standard technique.

Working into front loop of stitch (FLO)

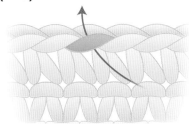

To work into the front loop of a stitch, pick up the front loop from underneath at the front of the work.

Working into back loop of stitch (BLO)

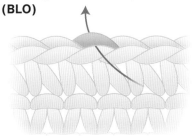

To work into the back loop of the stitch, insert the hook between the front and the back loop, picking up the back loop from the front of the work.

Single crochet (sc)

1. Insert the hook into your work, yarn over hook and pull the yarn through the work only. You will then have 2 loops on the hook.

2. Yarn over hook again and pull through the two loops on the hook. You will then have 1 loop on the hook.

Half double crochet (hdc)

  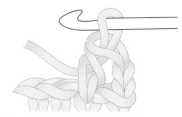

1. Before inserting the hook into the work, wrap the yarn over the hook and put the hook through the work with the yarn wrapped around.

2. Yarn over hook again and pull through the first loop on the hook. You now have 3 loops on the hook.

3. Yarn over hook and pull the yarn through all 3 loops. You will be left with 1 loop on the hook.

Double crochet (dc)

1. Before inserting the hook into the work, wrap the yarn over the hook. Put the hook through the work with the yarn wrapped around, yarn over hook again and pull through the first loop on the hook. You now have 3 loops on the hook.

2. Yarn over hook again, pull the yarn through the first 2 loops on the hook. You now have 2 loops on the hook.

3. Pull the yarn through 2 loops again. You will be left with 1 loop on the hook.

Treble crochet (tr)

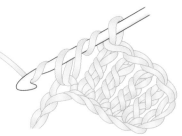

Yarn over hook twice, insert the hook into the stitch, yarn over hook, pull a loop through (4 loops on hook), yarn over hook, pull the yarn through 2 stitches (3 loops on hook), yarn over hook, pull a loop through the next 2 stitches (2 loops on hook), yarn over hook, pull a loop through the last 2 stitches. You will be left with 1 loop on the hook.

Double treble crochet (dtr)

Double trebles are "tall" stitches and are an extension on the basic treble stitch. They need a turning chain of 5 chains.

1. Yarn over hook three times, insert the hook into the stitch or space. Yarn over hook, pull the yarn through the work (5 loops on hook).

2. Yarn over hook, pull the yarn through the first 2 loops on the hook (4 loops on hook).

3. Yarn over hook, pull the yarn through the first 2 loops on the hook (3 loops on hook).

4. Yarn over hook, pull the yarn through the first 2 loops on the hook (2 loops on hook). Yarn over hook, pull the yarn through the 2 loops on the hook. You will be left with 1 loop on the hook.

Increasing

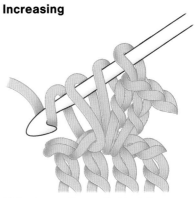

Make two or three stitches into one stitch or space from the previous row. The illustration shows a double crochet increase being made.

Decreasing

You can decrease by either missing the next stitch and continuing to crochet, or by crocheting two or more stitches together. The basic technique for crocheting stitches together is the same, no matter which stitch you are using.

Half double crochet two stitches together (hdc2tog)

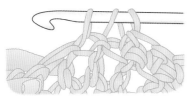 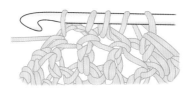 

1. Yarn over hook, insert hook into next stitch, yarn over hook, draw yarn through. You now have three loops on the hook.

2. Yarn over hook, insert hook into next stitch, yarn over hook, draw yarn through. This leaves five loops on the hook.

3. Draw the yarn through all five loops on the hook. You will then have one loop on the hook.

Single crochet two stitches together (sc2tog)

1. Insert the hook into your work, yarn over hook and pull the yarn through the work (2 loops on hook). Insert the hook in next stitch, yarn over hook and pull the yarn through.

2. Yarn over hook again and pull through all 3 loops on the hook. You will then have 1 loop on the hook.

Double crochet two stitches together (dc2tog)

 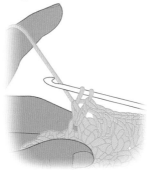 

1. Yarn over hook, insert the hook into the next space, yarn over hook, pull the yarn through the work (3 loops on hook).

2. Yarn over hook, pull the yarn through two loops on the hook (2 loops on hook).

3. Yarn over hook, insert the hook into the next space.

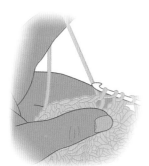  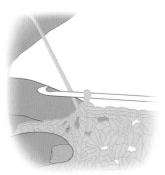

4. Yarn over hook, pull the yarn through the work (4 loops on hook).

5. Yarn over hook, pull the yarn through 2 loops on the hook (3 loops on hook).

6. Yarn over hook, pull the yarn through all 3 loops on the hook (1 loop on hook). One dc2tog (decrease) made.

Joining yarn at the end of a row or round

You can use this technique when changing color, or when joining in a new ball of yarn as one runs out.

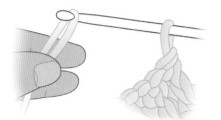

1. Keep the loop of the old yarn on the hook. Drop the tail and catch a loop of the strand of the new yarn with the crochet hook.

2. Draw the new yarn through the loop on the hook, keeping the old loop drawn tight and continue as instructed in the pattern.

Enclosing a yarn tail

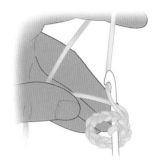

You may find that the yarn tail gets in the way as you work; you can enclose this into the stitches as you go by placing the tail at the back as you wrap the yarn. This also saves having to sew this tail end in later.

Fastening off

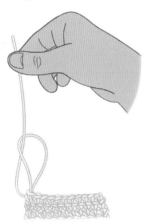

When you have finished crocheting, you need to fasten off the stitches to stop all your work unraveling.

Draw up the final loop of the last stitch to make it bigger. Cut the yarn, leaving a tail of approximately 4in (10cm)—unless a longer end is needed for sewing up. Pull the tail all the way through the loop and pull the loop up tightly.

Joining in new yarn after fastening off

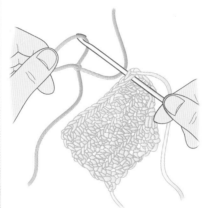

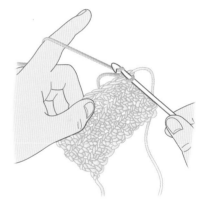

1. Fasten off the old color (see above). Make a slip knot with the new color (see page 117). Insert the hook into the stitch at the beginning of the next row, then through the slip knot.

2. Draw the loop of the slip knot through to the front of the work. Carry on working using the new color, following the instructions in the pattern.

Weaving in yarn ends

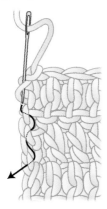

It is important to weave in the tail ends of the yarn so that they are secure and your crochet won't unravel. Thread a yarn needle with the tail end of yarn. On the wrong side, take the needle through the crochet one stitch down on the edge, then take it through the stitches, working in a gentle zigzag. Work through four or five stitches then return in the opposite direction. Remove the needle, pull the crochet gently to stretch it, and trim the end.

Blocking

Taking the time to block and stiffen a finished crochet project makes a huge difference to the finished effect of your work. Without either of these processes you will find that the crochet will curl out of shape and lose its definition.

For a quick and easy way to block your crochet you'll need blocking pins, some soft foam mats (such as the ones sold as children's play mats) and some ironing spray starch. Pin the crocheted piece out to shape and size on to the mats and then spray with the starch. Allow to dry for a day.

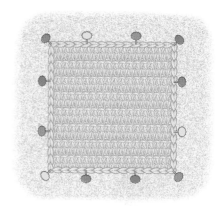

Making an oversewn seam

An oversewn join gives a nice flat seam and is the simplest and most common joining technique.

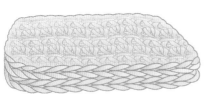

1. Thread a yarn sewing needle with the yarn you're using in the project. Place the pieces to be joined with right sides together.

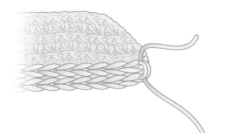

2. Insert the needle in one corner in the top loops of the stitches of both pieces and pull up the yarn, leaving a tail of about 2in (5cm). Go into the same place with the needle and pull up the yarn again; repeat two or three times to secure the yarn at the start of the seam.

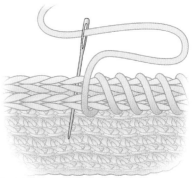

3. Join the pieces together by taking the needle through the loops at the top of corresponding stitches on each piece to the end. Fasten off the yarn at the end, as in step 2.

Sewing on buttons

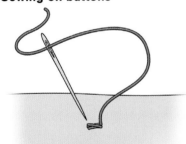

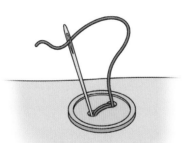

1. Mark the place where you want the button to go. Push the needle up from the back of the fabric and sew a few small stitches in this place.

2. Bring the needle up through one of the button's holes. Push the needle down through the second hole and the fabric. Bring it back up through the fabric and then the first hole. Repeat five or six times. Make sure you go up and down through the button's holes so the thread doesn't loop around the side of the button. If your button has four holes, use all four of them to make either a cross or parallel pattern. Finish with a few small stitches on the back of the crocheted fabric, and trim the thread.

Sewing on a bead

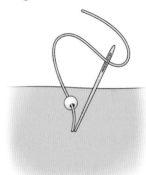

Bring the thread up through the fabric then thread on the bead. Take the thread over the bead and back down through the fabric.

crochet stitch conversion chart

Crochet stitches are worked in the same way in both the USA and the UK, but the stitch names are not the same and identical names are used for different stitches. On the right is a list of the US terms used in this book, and the equivalent UK terms.

USA term	UK term
single crochet (sc)	double crochet (dc)
half double crochet (hdc)	half treble (htr)
double crochet (dc)	treble (tr)
treble (tr)	double treble (dtr)
double treble (dtr)	triple treble (trtr)
gauge	tension
yarn over hook (yoh)	yarn round hook (yrh)

suppliers

USA

LoveCrafts
Online sales
www.lovecrafts.com

Knitting Fever Inc.
www.knittingfever.com

WEBS
www.yarn.com

Jo-Ann Fabric and Craft Stores
Yarns and craft supplies
www.joann.com

Michaels
Craft supplies
www.michaels.com

UK

LoveCrafts
Online sales
www.lovecrafts.com

Wool
Yarn, hooks
Store in Bath
+44 (0)1225 469144
www.woolbath.co.uk

Wool Warehouse
Online sales
www.woolwarehouse.co.uk

Laughing Hens
Online sales
Tel: +44 (0) 1829 740903
www.laughinghens.com

John Lewis
Yarns and craft supplies
Telephone numbers of stores
on website
www.johnlewis.com

Hobbycraft
Yarns and craft supplies
www.hobbycraft.co.uk

AUSTRALIA

Black Sheep Wool 'n' Wares
Retail store and online
Tel: +61 (0)2 6779 1196
www.blacksheepwool.com.au

Sun Spun
Retail store (Canterbury, Victoria)
and online
Tel: +61 (0)3 9830 1609
www.sunspun.com.au

index

a

abbreviations 8
animals
  Gray Rabbit 112–115
  Little Crab 28–29
  Parrot 20–21
  Pussy Cat 78–81
  Spider 106–107
Apple 76–77
Arrow Quiver 50–51

b

Basket 74–75
beads, sewing on 125
beards
  Pirate's Beard 14
  Wizard's Beard 110–111
blocking 124
buttons, sewing on 125

c

chain (ch) 117
chain ring 117
chain space (ch-sp) 118
Chest Plate 36–37
Cobweb Collar 102–103
collars
  Cobweb Collar 104–105
  Snowflake Collar 42–43
Corsage 59
Cowboy Carl (or Carla) 62–69
craft wire 8
cuffs
  Icicle Cuffs 44–45
  Superhero Cuffs 34–35
  Viking Cuffs 91
  Wrist Guards 52–53

d

decreasing 121–122
double crochet (dc) 120
double treble (dtr) 121

e

equipment 8
Eye Patch 15

f

Fairy Wings 60–61
Flower Garland 56–57
Forest Fairy 54–61

g

Gray Rabbit 112–115

h

hair
  Mermaid's Hair 24–25
  Rapunzel's Hair 94–95
half double crochet (hdc) 120
hats
  Cowboy Hat 64–65
  Mask 32–33
  Peaked Hat 48–49
  Pussy Cat Hat 80
  Rabbit Hat 114
  Tricorn Hat 16–17
  Viking Helmet 88–89
  Witch's Hat 100–101
  Wizard's Hat 110–111
Holster 66–67
Hooded Cape 72–73
hook
  holding the hook 116
  sizes 8
  yarn around hook 117
Horn Headdress 84–85

i

Icicle Cuffs 44–45
increasing 121

l

Little Crab 28–29
Little Mermaid 22–29

m

magic ring 117
Magic Unicorn 82–85
Mask 32–33

p

Parrot 20–21
Peaked Hat 48–49
Pete the Pirate 12–21
Pussy Cat 78–81

r

Rabbit Hat 114
Rapunzel 92–97
Red Riding Hood 70–77
Robin Hood 46–53
rounds, working in 118
rows, making 118

s

sewing up crochet 124
Sheriff's Badge 68–69
Shrug 98–99
single crochet (sc) 119
Skull & Crossbones Motif 18–19

slip knot 117
slip stitch (ss) 118
Snow Queen 38–45
Snowflake Collar 42–43
Snowflake Crown 40–41
Spider 104–105
stitch conversion chart 126
stitch marker 8
stitch techniques
  working into back loop of stitch 119
  working into front loop of stitch 119
  working into top of stitch 119
stitches
  double crochet (dc) 120
  double treble (dtr) 121
  half double crochet (hdc) 120
  single crochet (sc) 119
  slip stitch (ss) 118
  treble (tr) 120
Superhero 30–37

t

tails
  Magic Unicorn Tail 85
  Mermaid Tail 26–27
  Pussy Cat Tail 81
  Rabbit Tail 115
tapestry needle 8
techniques 116–125
Thor's Hammer 90
treble (tr) 120
Tricorn Hat 16–17

v

Vigo the Viking 86–91

w

Wicked Witch 98–105
Wily Wizard 106–111
Witch's Hat 100–101
Wizard's Hat 108–109
Wrist Guards 52–53

y

yarns 8
  holding the yarn 116
  joining new yarn 123
  small quantity 8
  weaving in yarn ends 124

acknowledgments

Compiling this book from patterns that were originally made just to be worn and played with has been such a fantastic experience. It's amazing that we can share them with other people and hopefully they'll be played with just as much too.

I'd like to thank Cindy Richards and Penny Craig at CICO for seeing the potential in what was essentially a pile of bonkers, woollen things; Rachel Atkinson for her sterling (and often challenging) work as editor, interpreting some of my frankly made up crochet techniques; and Zoe Clements for pattern checking so thoroughly.

I have to thank Neil, my husband, for encouraging me to write my patterns down in the first place, my beasts and nephews for all the inspiration—they are my muses—my horrible twin sister for the infernal unicorn, and the rest of my family for all their support. A special shout out has to go to the amazing Susannah for all her positivity and input, and an even bigger thank you to Freya for helping with all the girly things and trying stuff on.